THE FALL OF EBEN EMAEL

Belgium 1940

CHRIS McNAB

First published in Great Britain in 2013 by Osprey Publishing,
Midland House, West Way, Botley, Oxford, OX2 0PH, UK
43-01 21st Street, Suite 220B, Long Island City, NY 11101, USA
E-mail: info@ospreypublishing.com

Osprey Publishing is part of the Osprey Group

A CIP catalogue record for this book is available from the British Library

Print ISBN: 978 1 78096 261 0
PDF ebook ISBN: 978 1 78096 262 7
ePub ebook ISBN: 978 1 78096 263 4

Index by Sandra Shotter
Typeset in Sabon
Maps by bounford.com
3D BEV by Alan Gilliland
Originated by PDQ Media, Bungay, UK
Printed in China through Worldprint Ltd

13 14 15 16 17   10 9 8 7 6 5 4 3 2 1

Osprey Publishing is supporting the Woodland Trust, the UK's leading
woodland conservation charity, by funding the dedication of trees.

www.ospreypublishing.com

ARTIST'S NOTE

Readers may care to note that the original paintings from which the
battlescenes in this book were prepared are available for private sale. All
reproduction copyright whatsoever is retained by the Publishers. All
inquiries should be addressed to:

Peter Dennis, 'Fieldhead', The Park, Mansfield, Nottinghamshire NG18 2AT,
UK, or email magie.h@ntlworld.com

The Publishers regret that they can enter into no correspondence upon this
matter.

EDITOR'S NOTE

For ease of comparison please refer to the following conversion table:
1 mile = 1.6km
1yd = 0.9m
1ft = 0.3m
1in = 2.54cm/25.4mm
1 gallon (US) = 3.8 litres
1 ton (US) = 0.9 tonnes
1lb = 0.45kg

Fallschirmjäger	Belgian Army	US Army	British Army
Generalfeldmarschall	–	General of the Armies of the United States	Field marshal
Generaloberst	Général	General	General
General der Flieger	Lieutenant-général	Lieutenant general	Lieutenant general
Generalleutnant	Général-major	Major general	Major general
Generalmajor	Général de brigade	Brigadier General	Brigadier
Oberst	Colonel	Colonel	Colonel
Oberstleutnant	Lieutenant-colonel	Lieutenant colonel	Lieutenant colonel
Major	Major	Major	Major
–	Capitaine-commandant	–	–
Hauptmann	Capitaine	Captain	Captain
Oberleutnant	Lieutenant	1st lieutenant	1st lieutenant
Leutnant	Sous-lieutenant	2nd lieutenant	2nd lieutenant
Hauptfeldwebel	Adjudant	Warrant officer	Warrant officer
Oberfeldwebel	1e Sergent-major	Master sergeant	Colour sergeant major
Feldwebel	1e Sergent-chef	First sergeant	Staff sergeant
Unterfeldwebel	–	Technical sergeant	Sergeant
Oberjäger	1e Sergeant	Staff sergeant	–
Stabsgefreiter	Sergeant	Sergeant	–
Obergefreiter	Caporal	Corporal	Corporal
Gefreiter	1er Soldat	Private first class	Lance corporal
Jäger	Soldat	Private	Private

CONTENTS

INTRODUCTION   **4**
Airborne warriors   4

ORIGINS   **10**
Fall Gelb   11
The right force   14
The fort of Eben Emael   18

THE PLAN   **28**
Training begins   33

THE RAID   **38**
On the way   40
Coupole Nord   44
Mi-Sud and Mi-Nord   45
Maastricht 1 and Maastricht 2   48
Consolidating the attack   51
The bridges   56
Securing Eben Emael   63
Surrender   67

ANALYSIS   **70**
Lightning attack   73
The heroes   75

CONCLUSION   **77**

BIBLIOGRAPHY AND FURTHER READING   **79**

INDEX   **80**

INTRODUCTION

There are few better representations of elite soldiers or tactics in action than the raid on Eben Emael on 10 May 1940. Almost everything about the raid was cutting edge. The method of combat deployment – an airborne assault by glider-landed troops – was untested in action. The equipment carried by the Fallschirmjäger (paratroopers) included devastating new shaped-charge explosive devices, designed specifically to destroy armour and reinforced ferro-concrete emplacements. The unit itself was ground-breaking, as airborne troops were only just beginning to add a third (vertical) dimension to the practice of warfare.

Added to the technological and tactical innovations at Eben Emael was the sheer audacity of what was being attempted. Just 85 men of Sturmgruppe 'Granit' (Assault Group 'Granite') were assaulting one of the most powerful fortifications in the Western world, the objective covering 66 hectares (660,000m²), bristling with gun emplacements, and manned by a garrison of 1,200 Belgian troops. Despite the disparity in numbers and firepower, the small group of Germans were in control of the fort within a matter of hours. How they did so is one of the most compelling stories in military history.

Airborne warriors

The raid on Eben Emael was an early landmark in the development of an entirely new type of soldier – the airborne soldier. By the time the first man jumped from a fixed-wing aircraft in 1911, parachutes and parachuting had been under sketchy, often lethal, development for nearly five centuries. Credit over who took that first 1911 jump is uncertain; it is variously attributed to Americans Grant Morton or Captain Albert Berry. Others soon followed, but the rather traditionalist military community were at first non-committal, or even derisive, over the tactical potential of the parachute as a method of combat deployment.

This position began to change during World War I and the immediate years after the Armistice in 1918. In 1914, US female aerial adventurer

Georgia 'Tiny' Broadwick made several demonstration jumps for American government and military officials. Not only did she perform four static-line deployments, but she also stunned observers by making a freefall drop and living to tell the tale. Now the US military community at least was sitting up and paying attention to parachutes, if only because of the potential for the parachute to improve the survivability of its airmen. Yet in October 1918, with the end of World War I just a month away, the innovative US Army commander, Brigadier General William 'Billy' Mitchell (a passionate advocate of tactical airpower), proposed a radical way to conclude the fighting. The commander of the American Expeditionary Forces, General John Pershing, wanted to take the battle deep into the German heartland. The principal obstacle to this objective was Germany's superb defensive fortifications, particularly those integrated into the city of Metz. Mitchell's proposed solution was to deploy the entire US 1st Division from bombers via parachute, dropping them well behind the Metz positions. There they would hold fast until ground forces could move up and close the gap. This concept of 'vertical deployment' was not, for the time being, tested in practice, but the idea was revolutionary. By deploying troops from the air, using the distance-transcending qualities of aircraft, an army could place a force in the enemy's rear without the necessity of crossing his defensive lines. Once there they could attack their opponent's supply and communications infrastructure, force him to change his troop dispositions, and plunge him

A Fallschirmjäger makes a static-line parachute jump from a Ju 52 transport aircraft during a training exercise. This photo clearly illustrates the potential of 'vertical deployment' offered by the development of airborne warfare during the 1930s, principally by Germany, Italy and the Soviet Union. (Cody Images)

1 APRIL 1932

Construction work begins at the site for Eben Emael

into tactical uncertainty. There was also the potential for enveloping and attacking fortifications from directly above, typically a blind spot in many major fort systems.

Despite Mitchell's bold speculations, it wasn't until the 1920s and 1930s that actual units of airborne troops began to develop in earnest, during which decades it was the Europeans who took the lead. Several signal events changed the game, albeit in haphazard fashion. The first was undoubtedly the emergence of more effective long-range transport/bomber aircraft, such as the Italian Caproni Ca.73 (the paratroop transport version was known

This close-up of a German paratrooper illustrates the typical jump kit of the 1930s and early war years. In his left hand he clutches the hook that would attach to the static line inside the deployment aircraft; the parachute pack can be seen on his back. (Cody Images)

as the Ca.80S), the Soviet Tupolev TB-3 and the German Junkers Ju 52. The parachute was also going through refinements. In 1927 the Italian static-line 'Salvatore' parachute was introduced, offering paratroopers the ability to exit the aircraft quickly in tight 'sticks', concentrating them over the drop zone. Once allied to the British-developed quick-release harness, parachutes suddenly presented genuine tactical possibilities for the convenient deployment of airborne troops. At the same time, armies were also beginning to experiment with airlanding troops directly by aircraft, which offered the dimensional advantages of parachute deployment but without some of the physical risk and tactical dispersion.

While the Italians were arguably the first to form actual parachute units, doing so in the late 1920s, it was the Soviets of the 1930s who truly embraced the airborne principle. By 1931 the Red Army was performing small-unit parachute drops from converted bombers, but by 1933 airborne deployment was being conducted on regimental scale. Just two years later, the Soviets started to think big with manoeuvres in which 8,000 men were airlanded plus 3,000 paratroopers were dropped, along with associated light vehicles and equipments. Soviets were also working with glider-borne deployment methods as a more precise alternative to dropping men under wind-blown silk canopies.

By this time, Germany had also entered the airborne picture. Russia had become a convenient location for Germany to develop its military training and equipment away from the constraints imposed by the post-war Versailles Treaty. One man whose attention was immediately aroused by the sight of soldiers tumbling through the skies was the vainglorious commander-in-chief of the Luftwaffe, Hermann Göring, who had witnessed Soviet demonstrations in 1931 and 1935. With Heer (German Army) interest in parachute deployment distinctly lukewarm, Göring sensed an opportunity to steal a march. In 1933 Göring, in his other capacity as the chief of the Prussian police, had formed a small counter-terrorist unit known as Polizeiabteilung 'Wecke' (Police Detachment 'Wecke'), which also included a small parachute-deployable formation. The police detachment eventually swelled into the Regiment *General Göring*, and in the same month of its establishment – January 1936 – Göring provided a parachute demonstration for his soldiery, in an attempt to encourage them to join a new airborne battalion. He received 600 eager volunteers, and thus he established the Fallschirmschützen-Bataillon *Hermann Göring* (Parachute Soldiers Battalion 'Hermann Göring') under the command of Major Bruno Bräuer and trained at the new Luftwaffe Fallschirmjägerschule (Paratroop Training School) at the Stendal-Bostel airfield.

The Army's interest in airborne warfare was catching up fast. In the summer of 1936, the Oberkommando des Heeres (OKH; Army High Command) called for and received volunteers for a schwere-Fallschirm-Infanterie-Kompanie (Heavy Parachute Infantry Company). Then in 1937 the training of both Luftwaffe and Heer airborne troops was centralized at Stendal and headed by Major Gerhard Bassenge. More structural changes were afoot, however, as the Oberkommando der Wehrmacht (OKW; Armed

1933

First German parachute unit formed by Hermann Göring

Forces High Command) sought to rationalize the two branches of its emerging airborne force. The schwere-Fallschirm-Infanterie-Kompanie was upgraded to become the Fallschirm-Infanterie-Bataillon in April 1938, commanded by Major Richard Heidrich from its base in Braunschweig, at the same time as the Fallschirmschützen-Bataillon *Hermann Göring* became an independent battalion within a new parachute regiment – I Bataillon, Fallschirmjäger-Regiment Nr. 1 (I./FJR 1).

I./FJR 1 would form the kernel of a new German paratrooper division. Hitler had taken a personal interest in the emerging parachute arm of his military service, with his natural affinity for the concept of elite forces. Yet he also had a practical reason for developing the airborne arm further, as a strike force to take out Czech defensive positions in the coveted Sudetenland. To this end he ordered the establishment of an entire airborne division, to be commanded by Generalmajor Kurt Student, the head of the Münster Luftwaffe air district. (In January 1939 Student was also appointed as Inspekteur der Fallschirm- und Luftlandetruppen – Inspector of Parachute and Airlanding Troops.) In July 1938, 7. Flieger-Division was formed at Stendal but headquartered at Templehof near Berlin, and during 1939 – despite not having been required for Sudetenland operations – it grew rapidly. The Heer's parachute battalion was taken into the Luftwaffe as II./FJR 1 in January 1939, and in the following August Student began establishment of a third battalion for FJR 1 and the battalion nucleus of FJR 2. The Heer, meanwhile, had retained possession of an airlanding division, 22. Luftlande-Division (previously 22. Infanterie-Division), somewhat assuaging their chagrin at losing their paratroopers and providing a more flexible dimension to the Wehrmacht's offensive capability.

STUDENT ON AIRBORNE OPERATIONS

The operations of airborne forces provided for ground operations, which had hitherto been executable in two dimensions, the great advantage of the third dimension. Consequently, they brought with them the opportunity for military commands to simply jump over the enemy's front and hit the enemy in the rear, where and when they wanted. As is well known, an attack in the enemy's rear has always been the goal, since it is usually demoralizing and, therefore, the most effective. Airborne forces presented the opportunity to do that and were therefore of immeasurable value for the conduct of warfare.

In addition, there was the moment of surprise with the sudden appearance of an attack from paratroopers, which led to a paralyzing effect. The surprise becomes ever greater as more paratroopers jump into the enemy's territory. But therein alsolies the greatest danger for the jump-in force: The danger of landing too close to the enemy who is prepared to defend, and thereby experience an unpleasant surprise itself.

(Quoted in Kurowski 2010: 8)

In September 1939, Hitler's armed forces invaded Poland, setting in motion the rapid chain of events that led first to a European, then a global, war. Elements of 7. Flieger-Division, which was just one regiment plus one battalion (II./FJR 2) strong at the onset of hostilities, would participate in the earliest actions of World War II, primarily in focused security or airfield capture and defence operations. Poland collapsed within a month, but by the following November, and in great secrecy, Student and his commanders began planning their part in even larger operations in the West. Thus it was that Student oversaw the formation of an elite within an elite, known as Sturmabteilung 'Koch' (Assault Detachment 'Koch') and led by Hauptmann Walter Koch. They began to study, with great intensity, mapwork and models of the Belgian fortress of Eben Emael, and the nearby bridges over the Albert Canal. These men were now planning the operation that would introduce the world to the potential of airborne warfare.

ORIGINS

A modern-day view of the Caster cutting shows the scale of the engineering works required to construct the Albert Canal. The cutting through Montagne Saint-Pierre formed a sheer face on the northeastern side of the Eben Emael fortress, providing a natural defensive barrier against ground attack.
(Les Meloures)

In the smoking aftermath of World War I, the Belgian government and military took a long, hard look at the country's border defences, which had ultimately failed to stop the Germans in 1914. The attempts by the international community to contain and restrain Germany through the Versailles Treaty and various other strictures were less than successful, and tensions between Belgium and Germany remained high. German failures in its reparation schedule resulted in the Franco-Belgian occupation of the Ruhr in 1923.

Despite Belgium's budgetary austerity in the aftermath of the war, in 1926 the Belgian Minister of National Defence, M. de Broqueville, oversaw the creation of a commission to investigate rebuilding the country's border positions, many of which had been left in ruins by the war. In February 1927

the committee recommended the creation of the *Position Fortifée de Liège* (PFL), a chain of defences astride the river Meuse in the east. The rationale for the fortification system was made clear in a report by the newly formed Commission d'Étude du Système des Fortifications (Commission for the Study of National Fortification) on 28 January 1928:

> ... faced with the specific danger menacing the area near Maastricht where the Meuse leaves Belgian territory for eight kilometres of its length and where the enclave grows to a width of four kilometres west of the river and faced with the considerable extension of the lines of communication between Aix-la-Chapelle [Aachen] and Maastricht, the Commission has unanimously decided that ... all the main transportation roads and railways converging near Maastricht, the road leading out of the city and the enclave must be kept within the line of fire of permanent defensive artillery, capable of opening fire within seconds to avoid a surprise attack via Zuid Limburg [near Maastricht in the Netherlands] and all its consequences for the Liège defences.
>
> The commission has also agreed that these permanent armed defensive structures (estimated to contain a battery of four guns of 150 or 105mm) must be part of a larger line to be erected on the flanks of the Loën and that this group of structures must be supported by a permanent garrison ... (Quoted in Dunstan 2005: 9)

Realizing this vision on the ground would involve a combination of refurbishing old defences and creating new ones. The need for the establishment of such defences was clear, but its subsequent execution was not. Budget issues and political wrangles frequently dogged progress, but gradually a new and powerful line of Belgian emplacements emerged in earnest during the 1930s. Furthermore, on 30 May 1930 the Albert Canal, running 130km between Antwerp and Liège in Belgium, was given its inaugural ceremony and opened for canal traffic. The canal was not only a grand new waterway, it also provided a useful aquatic defensive barrier in the northeastern part of the country – memories of the Germans sweeping through this territory in 1914 were still keen. The vulnerable points in this line were the bridges that punctuated the canal at key points, and it was to protect these (rather than Liège itself, although Eben Emael was part of the PFL), plus turn an obstacle defence into a military one, that the fort of Eben Emael was constructed between 1932 and 1935.

Other forts were built and made operational between 1935 and 1940, when they would be tested by the German onslaught in the West. These included those at Boncelles, Embourg, Barchon, Battice, Wonck, Pontisse and Aubin Neufchâteau. Together their main guns (typically 75mm, 81mm and 120mm in calibre) formed overlapping fields of artillery fire that covered a 50km stretch of the Meuse, a guard against German penetration into the Belgian hinterland.

Fall Gelb

Hitler's invasion of Western Europe in May 1940, known as *Fall Gelb* (Case Yellow), required several pieces of a large and risky tactical jigsaw puzzle to fall neatly into place. The British and French were rightly expecting

Fallschirmjäger recruits perform jump training from the door of a mock-up Ju 52 transport aircraft. The poor design of the early German parachutes meant that landing was a precarious business, frequently resulting in ankle, knee or back injuries. (Cody Images)

that Hitler would eventually launch a campaign in the West; the only questions were in which locations and with what weighting of forces. The expectation, reinforced by past experience, was that the Germans would swing their main thrust down through Belgium and the Netherlands. Both of these countries were, by 1940, resolutely neutral. From September 1939 Belgium, despite its investment in border defences, clung to neutrality as the perceived best defence against German aggression, even to the extent of reinforcing its southern borders against possible incursions by the French. Nevertheless, intelligence sources were clear that the greatest threat lay to the east, so the garrisons occupying the fortifications of the PFL stood at high alert from the winter of 1939. (Hitler's original Western campaign date of November 1939 was postponed, the first of nearly 30 such postponements.)

The PFL was perceived by the British and the French as essential to the defence of the West (hence France had borne the bulk of the construction costs of Eben Emael in the 1930s). The defences on the Meuse and the Albert Canal might not stop the German juggernaut, but they could delay it long enough for British and French armies, concentrated in northern France, to push across the border and take up their own defensive lines between Antwerp and the Meuse. There they might provide a blocking force against the German advance, while admittedly weaker French formations guarded the Ardennes sector between the Maginot Line and Liège.

As history would later show, the Allied response plan actually played directly into Hitler's hands. His initial concept for the invasion of the West did indeed follow the line of a northern principal assault, essentially a modified version of the Schlieffen Plan that had been utilized in the opening stages of the World War I. During the many postponements of the plan from November 1939, however, the strategy changed significantly. The principal brain behind the shift was the illustrious German strategist Generalleutnant Erich von Manstein, Chief of Staff to Generaloberst Gerd von Rundstedt, the commander of the German Armeegruppe A (the army group allocated to the Ardennes sector of *Fall Gelb*). Known as *Sichelschnitt* ('Sickle-Slice'), von Manstein's modified plan switched the weight of focus to the attack through the Ardennes, wrongfooting the Allies as they pushed north to the Dyle Line in expectation of the major thrust through Belgium and the Netherlands.

Hitler was convinced by the daring plan, and it became the strategy that would bring such a great victory in May–June 1940. Yet even though the Ardennes was now the heart of the operation, the strike in the north, to be conducted by Generaloberst Fedor von Bock's Armeegruppe B, was still critical to success. It was this attack that would act as a northern lure to the Allied forces in France. The army group was to strike into the Netherlands and Belgium; 6. Armee under Generaloberst Walther von Reichenau was to

German infantry advance through Belgium in May 1940. Belgium's strict pre-war policy of neutrality did not ultimately protect the country from German aggression, and the Belgian Army did not receive the level of investment in weapons, armour and, above all, training enjoyed by the Wehrmacht. (Cody Images)

push straight across the Meuse at Maastricht and then take the key bridges across the Albert Canal at Veldwezelt, Vroenhoven and Kanne. Two points were central to this operation. First, the bridges had to be captured intact, otherwise the German thrust into Belgium would be seriously delayed. Second, Eben Emael – the guns of which covered much of 6. Armee's sector – had to be taken out of the fight quickly and decisively. The worst of all worlds for the Germans would be if their push was stopped dead by demolished bridges, under pounding artillery fire from the fortification.

The right force

During the early years of the Fallschirmjäger, there had been much debate about the appropriate tactical application of this emergent elite. Luftwaffe and Heer advocates of airborne warfare began to argue for rather different approaches. The Luftwaffe explored the possibilities of using paratroopers in 'destroyer' sections, small units dropped behind enemy lines to attack key targets, such as bridges, communication centres and railway junctions. Alternatively, the Heer looked at the airborne forces more in terms of large-scale infantry deployments, securing territory ahead of land advances. Interestingly, Student seems to have sided with the Heer perspective, although the operation at Eben Emael would have more of the 'destroyer' ethos.

Following the operations in Poland in 1939, the Fallschirmjäger focused their efforts on training for the campaign in the West. The expectation that each man would be a member of a true elite was reflected in the strenuous pace of training, the specialized instruction in airborne deployments and the use of distinctive weaponry. Before Fallschirmjäger training was decentralized later in the war, each paratrooper would spend eight weeks at Stendal, culminating in a 16-day parachute course. Much of the early stages of the training was a bone-wearying test of endurance, conducted through route marches, parade drill, assault courses and unarmed combat instruction. Infantry training was introduced with tactical exercises from Gruppe to battalion levels, the purpose being as much about breeding a unit *esprit d'corps* as it was about creating a tactically functional body of men.

The parachute part of the training separated the Fallschirmjäger from all other soldiers in the Wehrmacht. The first few days were given to practising the correct packing, wearing and use of the Rüchenpackung Zwangauslösung 1 (RZ 1) and RZ 16 parachute from the doorway of a Ju 52 transport aircraft. It should be noted – as it had a bearing on the deployment method finally chosen at Eben Emael – that the German parachutes left much to be desired in terms of design. The static-line Salvatore-style RZ parachutes required a rather alarming head-first dive from the aircraft; if the para wasn't in a head-first vertical position at the time of canopy opening he risked serious deceleration injuries. Also the behind-the-shoulders positioning of the canopy shrouds and their web attachments to the harness meant that the soldiers actually had no control over rotation or the direction of their drop. In other words, they went where the wind took them. Even with deployment in a tight group over the target area, and from low altitudes of around 150m, para dispersal was therefore extremely high – a typical

group of 12 paratroopers would be spread over an area of 900m², even if they performed their jump with clockwork-like precision. The lack of control over the landing also produced a high percentage of injuries on impact with the ground, as the Fallschirmjäger later found to their high cost over the rocky terrain of Crete in May 1941.

It took six of these nerve-testing leaps of faith before a Fallschirmjäger was granted his *Fallschirmschützenabzeichen* (Parachutist's Badge), and entered the elite ranks of airborne forces. The new para looked and thought in very different ways to the general run of German infantry. His appearance, in operational terms anyway, was defined by the thigh-length all-in-one jump smock, and the cut-down *Fallschirmhelm* (paratrooper's helmet) – the earpieces of the regular German steel helmet were cut away (or later omitted in the manufacturing process) to avoid their getting caught

A German para demonstrates the correct vertical jump profile during a training exercise, his ripcord snaking back to the static line inside the aircraft. Another para waits to make his jump in the doorway of the Ju 52, his hands braced either side of the door to achieve a forceful jump. (Cody Images)

THE FALLSCHIRMJÄGER TEN COMMANDMENTS

- You are the elite of the Wehrmacht. For you, combat shall be fulfilment. You shall seek it out and train yourself to stand any test.

- Cultivate true comradeship, for together with your comrades you will triumph or die.

- Be shy of speech and incorruptible. Men act, women chatter; chatter will bring you to the grave.

- Calm and caution, vigour and determination, valour and a fanatical offensive spirit will make you superior in attack.

- In facing the foe, ammunition is the most precious thing. He who shoots uselessly, merely to reassure himself, is a man without guts. He is a weakling and does not deserve the title of paratrooper.

- Never surrender. Your honour lies in Victory or Death.

- Only with good weapons can you have success. So look after them on the principle – first my weapons, then myself.

- You must grasp the full meaning of an operation so that, should your leader fall by the way, you can carry it out with coolness and caution.

- Fight chivalrously against an honest foe; armed irregulars deserve no quarter.

- Keep your eyes wide open. Tune yourself to the top-most pitch. Be nimble as a greyhound, as tough as leather, as hard as Krupp steel and so you shall be the German warrior incarnate. (Quoted in Anon 1943)

up in the parachute lines during jumps. High black jump boots laced all the way up to the calves.

The weapons of the Fallschirmjäger included the familiar German hardware of the Wehrmacht – the Kar 98k carbine and MP 38/MP 40 submachine gun, plus the MG 34 as the squad- and platoon-level support weapon. (Note that the Fallschirmjäger typically had a higher proportion of automatic weapons compared to equivalent Heer units, as during airborne operations they would often have to operate without the benefit of large-scale support weapons.) They also took into action the standard flamethrowers and mortars. There were some specialist adaptations of the regular weapons, however (notwithstanding the late-war para-specific firearms, such as the Fallschirmjägergewehr 42 automatic rifle). There were carbine versions of infantry rifles, such as the Brünn Gew 33/40(t), and the paras also utilized a variety of pistols, including the Luger Pistole 08 and the Sauer 7.65mm Modell 38(H) pistol. At the heavier end of the scale, the Fallschirmjäger also developed a series of light air-portable anti-tank guns, but many of these were not yet available at the time of the Eben Emael raid.

One issue that made life additionally fraught for the Fallschirmjäger was that the mode of parachute deployment made it hard to carry anything larger than a pistol and a few hand grenades during the actual parachute drop. The majority of the weaponry and ammunition was therefore carried

in special drop containers, thrown out on their own parachutes alongside the soldiers as they jumped. This unfortunately meant that until the para could find the container and retrieve his firearms, he was largely helpless. Many paras did end up jumping holding carbines or submachine guns, but they had an additional risk of injury upon landing.

Despite the issues surrounding airborne deployment, the Fallschirmjäger began to prove their true operational worth in the German invasion of Denmark and Norway in April 1940. Major Erich Walther's I./FJR 1, four companies strong, was given a range of high-priority targets to be captured following parachute deployment, and to be held until airlanded forces could be deployed in strength. Many of the objectives were airfields – Fornebu-Oslo, Sola-Stavanger and two at Aalborg (II./FJR 2 conducted a defence of Trondheim-Vaernes airbase in June) – but other challenges for the paras included securing the causeway linking Falster and Seeland and a drop at the vital railway junction near Dombas, the paras there intending to perform a blocking action against British forces pushing south from Aandalesnes.

The Scandinavian operations brought somewhat mixed results. The Falster–Seeland causeway and the Aalborg airbases fell to the Fallschirmjäger with virtually no casualties; in many cases the local defenders were too stunned by the sight of foreign soldiers falling from the skies to put up much of a fight. The airbases were taken by a platoon of men in just 30 minutes, and within two hours the Luftwaffe had made them operational. This was a perfect example of the Fallschirmjäger concept in action, but elsewhere the German airborne troops had a far rougher ride. The assault on Sola-Stavanger airfield, for example, was dogged even on the approach by bad weather, and only a convenient gap in the Scandinavian gloom allowed the men of

A later-war para squad leader, his command role indicated by the 6×30 binoculars hanging around his neck. Airborne NCOs were trained to take over responsibility for a mission in the absence (through death, injury or other cause) of officers, hence the tactical excellence of the Fallschirmjäger. (Note the MP 40 submachine-gun magazine pouches on the belt.) (Cody Images)

3. Kompanie, Fallschirmjäger-Regiment 1 (3./FJR 1) to jump at all. On the way down, the men were met by heavy fire, and once on the ground they were separated from their weapons containers for about half an hour, during which time they took mounting casualties. Only with the addition of airlanded troops was the airfield secured.

A worse situation faced Oberleutnant Schmidt's action at Dombas. The appalling weather forced the drop to be made at unacceptably low altitudes; many paras were killed or injured when their parachutes failed to open properly, and others died quickly at the landing zone from incoming fire. Effectively cut off from support by weather and circumstance, the remaining members of the company fought on for no less than five days, while food and ammunition steadily ran out. Eventually Schmidt, himself suffering from two wounds, surrendered his battered men to the Norwegians. Thankfully for these paras, the German occupation of Norway meant that they would not stay in captivity for long.

Although the Scandinavian airborne operations illustrated the precarious nature of airborne operations, and also highlighted serious issues with the deployment of men and weapons together by parachute, the operations were largely heralded as successes. It was evident that the Fallschirmjäger could perform decisive vertical assaults against localized targets. It was therefore unsurprising that the airborne forces were selected for the forthcoming operation against Eben Emael. The action against this fortress required shock, speed, tactical talent and a ruthlessly focused attitude, and the Fallschirmjäger had these qualities in abundance.

The fort of Eben Emael

Eben Emael was not a fortress in a commonplace sense of a unitary above-ground building. Instead it was a system of ferro-concrete gun emplacements, bunkers, pillboxes and blockhouses at ground level, supplied and garrisoned from an extensive network of subterranean interconnecting tunnels and buildings. The site, sat on elevated ground 120m above the Albert Canal, described a rough diamond shape oriented on a north–south axis, being about 900m long and, at its widest point, 700m wide. One of its greatest defensive strengths, however, was its location. The excavation of the Albert Canal involved cutting straight through the 120m-high Montagne Saint-Pierre ridge running north to south between the Geer and Meuse rivers. The resulting 1,300m-long Caster cutting was one of the most impressive engineering accomplishments of the early 20th century. The cutting formed the northeastern perimeter of Eben Emael, and it was a formidable obstacle to ground troops advancing from that direction. On the western side of the fort was a massive anti-tank ditch measuring 450m long by 10m wide, which could be filled with water from the nearby river Geer (the ditch was concrete-lined to prevent the water soaking away into the ground). A similar anti-tank ditch also ran around the southern edge of Eben Emael.

All of the ditches and the fortress section of the Caster cutting were covered by blockhouses, these being hefty ferro-concrete structures armed with anti-tank artillery pieces and machine guns. There were seven blockhouses in total dotted around the perimeter of the fortress, the fields of fire offered by each overlapping with those adjacent, thereby delivering a 360-degree defence against direct ground assault. Bloc 1 was two storeys high and functioned as an entrance to the fortress at the southwestern tip; it possessed two 60mm anti-tank guns and three machine guns. (The standard machine guns used in Belgian fortifications were 7.65mm versions of the Maxim MG 08 and MG 08/15, and the 7.65mm Fusil-Mitrailleur 1930 (FM 30), a Belgian version of the Browning Automatic Rifle/BAR.) Bloc 1 included an armoured observation dome on the top for fire-direction personnel. This dome had an armour thickness of 20cm, with observation provided through four observation slits filled with armoured glass. This dome, and the others elsewhere in the fortress, could not only shrug off small-arms fire, but also proximate artillery explosions. A heavy gate guarded the roadway that ran through the blockhouse into the fortress, and a 4m section of the roadway was itself retractable, which when lifted would stop anyone attempting to enter the fortress and trap them in a concentrated killing zone. Near Bloc 1 was also a collection of administrative, utility and personnel buildings, including latrines, generators, a kitchen, food storeroom, barber's shop, hospital, operating theatre and dental surgery.

Bloc 2 sat on the western anti-tank ditch, and was armed and equipped in the same fashion as Bloc 1, including an armoured observation dome. It also had a similar garrison: four NCOs and 22 soldiers, as compared to Bloc 1's five NCOs and 23 soldiers. One distinctive feature of Bloc 2 was a sally port, which allowed its occupants to make quick counter-attacks into the surrounding area, then retreat quickly back to the safety of the bunker.

On the Albert Canal side of the fortification, actually built into the cutting wall, were two more blockhouses, known as Canal Nord and Canal Sud. (There was no Bloc 3.) Each of these positions had one 60mm anti-tank gun plus three machine guns, and featured observation domes with firing ports

The entrance to Eben Emael – Bloc 1 – as it stands today, still showing the shrapnel and bullet scars of war from more than 70 years ago. During the battle of 1940, the position was bombed heavily by Ju 87 dive-bombers, although the structure was not breached. (Huile)

for machine guns and flare guns, plus searchlights to illuminate the canal in case of an attempted amphibious night crossing. Crew strength of each of these positions was three NCOs and 17 men.

Moving to the southeastern side of the fortress, here we find Bloc 4, with two 60mm anti-tank guns, two machine guns, two searchlights and an armoured observation dome. It was manned by four NCOs and 22 soldiers. As well as covering the anti-tank ditch on this aspect of the approach to the fortress, Bloc 4 had fields of fire that intersected with those of Bloc 5 on the southeastern tip, which in turn intersected with the weapons of Bloc 6 at the southwestern corner. Bloc 5, which had a garrison of three NCOs and 14 soldiers, was not only armed with a searchlight, a 60mm anti-tank gun and two machine guns, but was surmounted by Coupole Sud, a retractable

The Maastricht 2 gun emplacement, with the EBEN 3 armoured cupola on its roof, this feature offering protected observation over the Albert Canal. The three embrasures held 75mm quick-firing cannon, and the gun on the left was destroyed in the battle by a 12.5kg shaped charge. (Wasily)

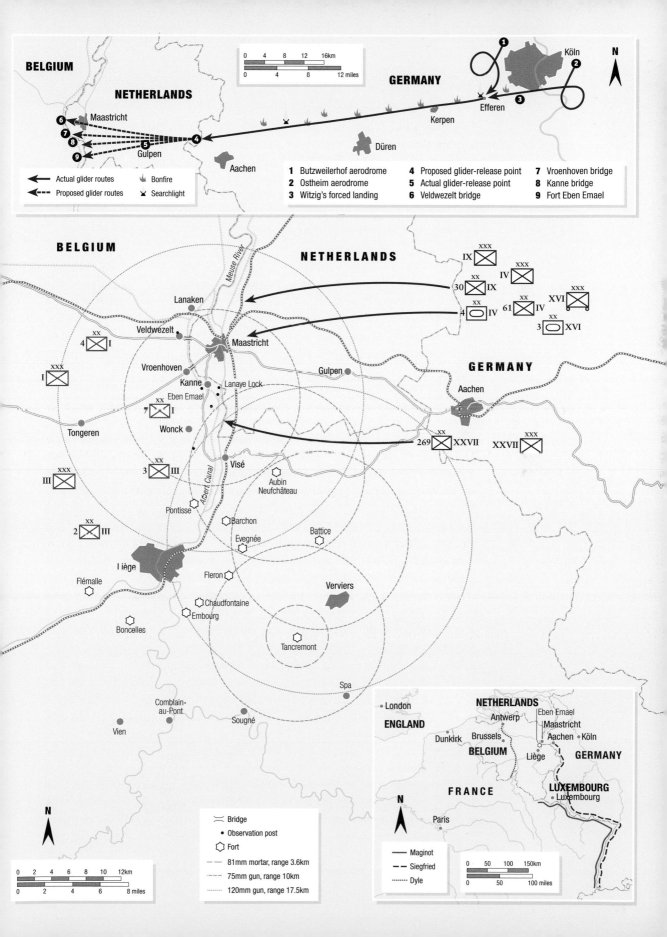

Top map

BELGIUM

NETHERLANDS

GERMANY

Köln

Efferen

Kerpen

Düren

Maastricht

Gulpen

Aachen

Actual glider routes
Proposed glider routes
Bonfire
Searchlight

1 Butzweilerhof aerodrome
2 Ostheim aerodrome
3 Witzig's forced landing
4 Proposed glider-release point
5 Actual glider-release point
6 Veldwezelt bridge
7 Vroenhoven bridge
8 Kanne bridge
9 Fort Eben Emael

0 4 8 12 16km
0 4 8 12 miles

N

Main map

BELGIUM

NETHERLANDS

GERMANY

Meuse River

IX XXX
30 IX XXX
4 IV
IV XXX
61 IV XXX
XVI XXX
3 XVI

Lanaken

Veldwezelt

Maastricht

4 XX I

Vroenhoven

Kanne

Lanaye Lock

Eben Emael

7 XX I

Wonck

Gulpen

Aachen

I XXX

Tongeren

3 XX III

Visé

Aubin Neufchâteau

269 XX XXVII

XXVII XXX

III XXX

2 XX III

Pontisse

Albert Canal

Barchon

Evegnée

Battice

Liège

Fleron

Verviers

Flémalle

Chaudfontaine

Embourg

Boncelles

Tancremont

Spa

Comblain-au-Pont

Sougné

Vien

N

0 2 4 6 8 10 12km
0 2 4 6 8 miles

>< Bridge
• Observation post
⬡ Fort
- - - 81mm mortar, range 3.6km
– – – 75mm gun, range 10km
······ 120mm gun, range 17.5km

Inset map

ENGLAND
London

NETHERLANDS
Antwerp
Eben Emael
Maastricht
Aachen · Köln

Dunkirk
Brussels
BELGIUM
Liège
GERMANY

FRANCE
LUXEMBOURG
Luxembourg

Paris

N

—— Maginot
– – – Siegfried
······ Dyle

0 50 100 150km
0 50 100 miles

gun emplacement (see below). Bloc 6 (three NCOs and 17 soldiers), meanwhile, had two 60mm anti-tank guns, two machine guns, a searchlight and an armoured observation dome. Note that the C 60 L/50 60mm anti-tank gun, when mounted in fortresses, was often equipped with high-explosive shells rather than armour-piercing ammunition, and even had its sights modified for indirect fire rather than anti-armour direct fire.

Thus ran the perimeter defence of Eben Emael. The true power and purpose of the fortification, however, lay in its main gun batteries, set in armoured emplacements dotted around the site. The principal weapons of these emplacements, apart from secondary machine-gun defence, were the FRC Modèle 1934 75mm and, in far more limited numbers, the FRC Modèle 31 120mm gun. The 75mm weapon was valued not only for its useful range of 11km (depending on ammunition type) – meaning that from Eben Emael it could reach out to strike a couple of kilometres north of Maastricht or south of Visé – but also its rapid-fire capabilities. In the dextrous hands of a seasoned gun crew, the 75mm was capable of firing 25 rounds per minute, although a more typical cyclical rate was in the region of 15 rounds. (The cyclical rates of fire at Eben Emael naturally varied according to factors such as the rate of ammunition supply and targeting adjustments.) In addition to conventional high-explosive rounds, the gun could also fire fearsome short-range anti-personnel canister rounds, each shell lashing the ground in front of the muzzle with 205 1.5cm-diameter lead balls, and to a range of 200m. The 120mm guns naturally traded its slower rate of fire against longer reach and more devastating terminal effects. Simon Dunstan, in his study of the fortress at Eben Emael, notes that 'these powerful weapons required periodic cooling during sustained fire missions, and there was no provision for water-cooling. Accordingly, the rate of fire was notionally restricted to no more than two rounds per minute for the first five minutes and one round every 40 seconds for the next 15 minutes' (Dunstan 2005: 28).

Not the most impressive rate of fire. Yet the 120mm guns were part of the total package of firepower offered by Eben Emael, alongside the 60mm and 75mm weapons (plus numerous small arms), and it rounded off the fire capabilities of the fortress proficiently. The 120mm had a reach of 17.5km, able to punch from Eben Emael well into the Netherlands and almost touch Liège in the south. It could even drop shells less than 5km from the German border. (The 120mm guns at the fortress of Battice to the southeast could actually touch this border.) Therefore, not only could the 120mm gun inflict long-range attrition on the enemy, it could also engage in brutal counter-battery fire against most heavy siege artillery pieces that might be brought against the fort.

There were several forms of emplacement designed for these guns at Eben Emael. The Maastricht 1, Maastricht 2, Visé 1 and Visé 2 emplacements were massive casemates formed from reinforced concrete 2.75m thick, impervious to most heavy artillery shells and aerial bomb strikes. Two of the emplacements – Maastricht 1 and Visé 2 – were also partially built into the landscape of the fortress roof, the earth providing an additional layer of blast-absorbing protection. Each of these four casemates contained three 75mm guns, their muzzles jutting from recessed apertures in the face of the position. The guns themselves were positioned in the upper floor of the casemate, along with the telephonists who received and relayed fire orders from the fortress command post. (Maastricht 2 also had a large armoured observation dome on top, known as EBEN 3, which allowed it more direct observation of its target areas.) The lower floor consisted of the ammunition room; lifts were used to take the ammunition from this room to the floor above. Each of the four emplacements had garrisons of five NCOs and 28 soldiers, although Maastricht 2 had an additional three personnel in EBEN 3.

In terms of location, Maastricht 1 was positioned in the southern area of the fortress, while Maastricht 2 was a short distance away in the western lower half. Visé 2 sat low down in the southern end, while Visé 1 occupied an opposite position near the edge of the Caster cutting. As the names of these emplacements connotes, their purpose was to deliver fire in the direction of Maastricht and Visé respectively. The Maastricht guns in particular had the important bridges at Kanne, Vroenhoven and Veldwezelt in their sights. All of the guns could target potential crossing areas over the Meuse, plus rain fire down on major highways between the Meuse and the Dutch/German border.

Also equipped with the redoubtable 75mm guns were Coupole Nord and Coupole Sud positioned respectively in the southeast and southern tip of the fortress. Yet these positions were very different in nature to the triple-gun emplacements. Each held two 75mm guns in retractable armoured cupolas, each cupola rising half a metre out of the ground when the guns were in action. In this position the cupola could also be rotated through 360 degrees, and trained in any direction. When the cupola was retracted, all that remained above ground was an immensely strong curved shell consisting of 38cm-thick steel armour. As additional layers of protection for the crew inside (three NCOs and 22 soldiers), the cupolas also incorporated special shockwave reduction structures and were even sealed against gas attack. Coupole Nord also had a machine gun for defence against infantry attack.

One of the most striking of the emplacements at Eben Emael was Coupole 120, armed with two 120mm guns and crewed by four NCOs and 24 soldiers. This massive but non-retractable cupola weighed no less than 230 tonnes, with 210 tonnes of armour plate over the gunroom it protected (Dunstan 2005: 26). Despite its great mass, it could also rotate through 360 degrees, the hydraulic pumps to achieve this located on the second of the emplacement's three floors. (The top floor was the gunroom, while the bottom floor was an ammunition collection and distribution point, the shells fed to the gunroom by hoists.) Coupole 120 was the mightiest of Eben Emael's weapon systems.

At the lighter end of Eben Emael's emplacements were Mi-Nord and Mi-Sud, both located in the upper part of the fortress's diamond. Unlike the aforementioned 75mm casemates, these positions were equipped purely with double machine guns, three sets each (the 'Mi' abbreviation stood for

Coupole Sud, the armoured and retractable cupola atop Bloc 5, was armed with twin 75mm guns. The cupola proved to be one of the most durable emplacements of the battle of Eben Emael, remaining active for most of the two-day battle. (Wasily)

mitrailleuse, or machine gun). Both had an armoured observation dome on top, manned by a crew of three and incorporating a revolving telescope. The three sets of double machine guns used in each of these positions gave, through their arrangement to deliver mutually supporting fire, a powerful internal defence mechanism, should anyone manage to gain access to the fortress roof. Mi-Nord was manned by three NCOs and 12 soldiers, while

IMPREGNABLE FORTRESS

Here Colonel Albert Torreele, a Belgian infantry officer, recalls his impressions of Eben Emael following a visit there in 1938:

'An officer of the garrison of the fort led us to many of the outer defences and showed what each was intended for. We went to the walls and looked over the countless rows of barbed wire. He led us to the only door on the surface set deep in the concrete. It appeared like the heavy steel door of a bank vault. From here [Coupole Nord] infantry in reserve would issue to repel any enemy fortunate to get by the tough ground defences.

He took us deep into the interior and we trudged many miles to the end of the tunnels, visiting the crews and the guns of the emplacements we had seen on the surface. Crews gave us their missions and detailed characteristics of their guns. All was very professional. Later, we assembled in the command post. The commandant gave a detailed account of how he proposed to defend the fort in the event of an attack. I got the impression of tremendous power and first-rate efficiency. I was convinced nothing could happen!' (Quoted in Dunstan 2005: 32)

INSIDE THE 75MM CASEMATES

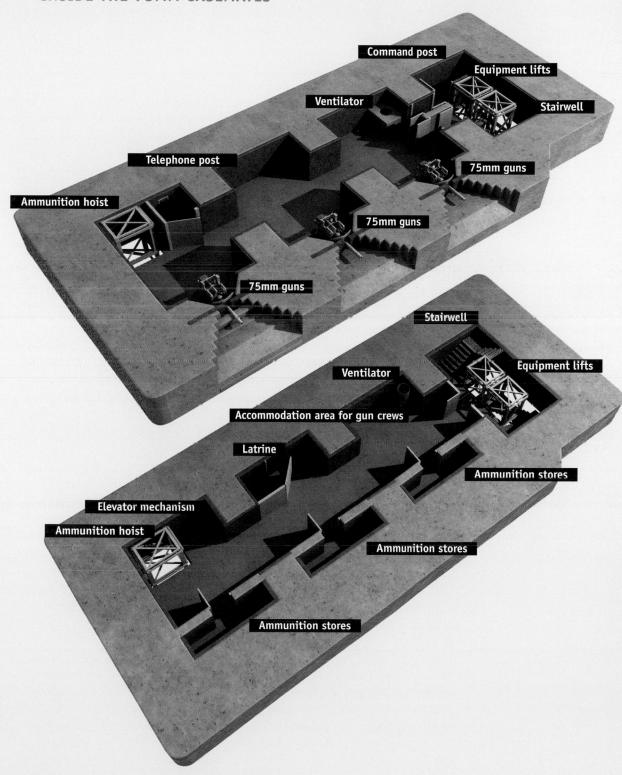

Command post

Equipment lifts

Ventilator

Stairwell

Telephone post

75mm guns

Ammunition hoist

75mm guns

75mm guns

Stairwell

Ventilator

Equipment lifts

Accommodation area for gun crews

Latrine

Ammunition stores

Elevator mechanism

Ammunition hoist

Ammunition stores

Ammunition stores

Mi-Sud had the same number of NCOs but 11 soldiers. Anti-aircraft defence came in the form of the *Mitrailleuse contre avions* (MICA), consisting of four 7.65mm Maxim guns closely grouped in single-gun emplacements. The Belgian designers, with one eye open to the realities of aerial reconnaissance, also emplaced three false cupolas around the fortress, to confuse those who might be making plans to attack.

We have already noted some of the observation features of Eben Emael, particularly the observation domes atop Mi-Nord (EBEN 2) and Maastricht 2 (EBEN 3). Fortresses always run the risk of being blind to critical avenues of approach, particularly when the garrison is hunkered down in casemates offering limited visibility, or deep underground in subterranean positions. Various further observation positions, therefore, were located both within and outside Eben Emael, multiplying the eyes over the fortress and the surrounding countryside and waterways, and taking advantage of the elevated position offered by the landscape. Southwest of the fortress perimeter, on the bank of the Albert Canal, was Bloc 01 (not to be confused with Bloc 1), surmounted by the armoured observation dome EBEN 1. Dunstan notes that 'From its dominating position, Bloc 01 was able to observe all movement over a wide area as far south as Visé and thus provide fire missions for Visé 1 and Visé 2 as well as Coupoles 120, Nord and Sud as necessary' (Dunstan 2005: 30). Bloc 01 was also capable of conducting its own defence, being equipped with a 60mm anti-tank gun, three machine guns and three searchlights. Numerous other observation posts sat at key points in the vicinity of Eben Emael, while inside the fortress itself there was also the more rudimentary precaution of 14 two-man observation foxholes, set high up on the fortress's terrain, to act as unprotected pairs of eyes should the fortress come under attack.

The garrison and the fort below ground

So far we have simply focused on the external features of Eben Emael, or the below-ground structures immediately supporting them. Yet the fortress had a thriving subterranean life, with more than 9km of tunnels linking the various emplacements and positions. The fortress was divided into two basic levels. The intermediate level was concerned principally with ammunition supply and fire control, and 4km of tunnels on this level linked together all the various gun positions. Access to this level was restricted by armoured doors and a staircase that descended 21m down into the earth; elevators were also used, although these were restricted to use by officers and for ammunition supply only. In addition to the fort's *post de commandement* (command post), which distributed fire orders to the gun crews above, the level contained the magazines for each emplacement. In all, the magazines contained 19,200 75mm rounds, 6,000 60mm, and 2,000 120mm. The broad dispersal of the magazines – there was at least 150m of corridors and passageways between each magazine – was a lesson hard learnt from the fighting of World War I. Separating each casemate from the fortress interior were double pairs of massive armoured doors, the 2m gap between each set of doors further blocked, in times of crisis, with a steel girder barrier and sandbags (the latter to absorb explosive force if an enemy attempted to blast through the doors). The effect was that the crew of an out-of-action emplacement could scuttle through the double doors, erecting the obstacles and locking the doors on the way through, and consequently create a barrier virtually impervious to enemy penetration. To make the intermediate level doubly hostile to invaders, machine-gun posts with weapons mounted in armoured embrasures commanded the passageways at various points. One final point to note about the intermediate level was that it also contained major inlets for the fort's ventilation system, these being located on the side of the Caster cutting, from which clean air could be pumped into the interior.

The ground floor of the fort was devoted more to the essential life-support systems of the fortress. As well as a hospital, the level also included a water-purification system (the fortress had its own internal well), barracks for the soldiery, air conditioning and decontamination systems. Although the fortress was ventilated to acceptable levels, the atmosphere deep inside Eben Emael could, in places, be less than wholesome, with damp, dark corridors and claustrophobic accommodation.

The garrison of Eben Emael was, arguably, one of its weakest links. Although the fortress had powerful defensive systems in place, its manpower was largely composed of artillery, support and administrative personnel. This composition meant that its capability to perform a tactical defence at close quarters was relatively poor, regardless of what systems of defence it had in place. At full strength the garrison numbered 1,322 men, although on 9 May 1940 the garrison numbered 1,198. (In peacetime, the typical active complement of the fortress was about 750.) Of these people, around 500 were artillery crew, and the remainder support/administrative staff. In turn, the artillerymen were organized into two notional batteries. The 1er Batterie took charge of all the long-range guns within the main fortress plateau, while the 2e Batterie was responsible for the perimeter defensive weapons. Major Jean Fritz Lucien Jottrand served as the commander at the time of the raid.

Even taking into account some of the limitations of the garrison who manned Eben Emael, there was no doubting the daunting force and the tactical challenge the fortress presented to even a determined enemy. A combination of numerous interlocking fields of fire, heavily armoured emplacements, intelligently mixed weaponry and ammunition types, a precipitous physical location, armour-resistant perimeter defences, plus numerous other combative measures, meant that Eben Emael was amongst the most formidable fortifications in the world in May 1940. It was with this evident fact in mind that Adolf Hitler summoned Kurt Student to the Reichskanzlei (Reich Chancellery) on 27 October 1939.

THE PLAN

OCTOBER 1939

Planning begins for the operation against Eben Emael

History has left a rather distorted picture of Adolf Hitler as a tactician. His command behaviour from late 1942 onwards shows a mind in a disintegrating relation to reality, steadily losing pragmatic understanding of battlefield conditions and the formations under his control. By 1945, his handling of his armies was little short of shambolic, and it doubtless contributed to the eventual Allied defeat of Nazi Germany. Yet in the early years of the war, Hitler did demonstrate consistent flashes of tactical brilliance, even if these were darkened by the ideological horror of what he aimed to achieve. The plan to raid Eben Emael is one such case.

It was clear to Hitler and his staff that taking Eben Emael was a priority for the opening moves of *Fall Gelb*, as was the need to secure the crucial bridges over the Albert Canal. Equally clear, however, was that conventional options for taking the fortress were limited. An assault by armour and infantry at ground level was likely to be torn up by the fortress's artillery, even before the attack could actually attempt to negotiate the problematic anti-tank ditches. A lengthy reduction of the fortress by siege was not an option; what we now know as *Blitzkrieg* (lightning war) relied upon rapid penetrations and movement to achieve its goals, not protracted attrition. Furthermore, the armoured resilience of Eben Emael meant that it could ride out the worst punishment from air and artillery bombardment, while also returning heavy counter-battery fire.

Vertical deployment by airborne forces offered itself as the most innovative and viable way to assault Eben Emael. The Fallschirmjäger could be deployed directly into the fortification, rather than having to batter their way into it like ground troops. Airborne warfare was also in its absolute infancy – the surprise factor alone could be decisive, paralyzing the enemy response from the outset. The issue with using the Fallschirmjäger, however, revolved around two principal problems – deployment and weaponry.

As we have already noted, parachute deployment had some wayward characteristics, especially when the weather was unfavourable. Even though

A light-hearted photograph of Rudolf Witzig, the commander of Sturmgruppe 'Granit'. Witzig was just 24 years old at the time of the Eben Emael raid, having joined the Heer in 1935 and qualifying as a parachutist in 1938. A glider mishap meant he wasn't present for the initial phases of the assault. (Cody Images)

Eben Emael was a large fortification, it was still a rather small area in which to concentrate a large group of paratroopers and all their equipment. Even if the paratroopers could drop successfully onto the fortress roof, if their weapons containers landed elsewhere they could be cut to pieces by canister rounds and machine-gun fire before they had a chance to really get into the fight. Furthermore, there was the vexing problem of how lightly armed paratroopers could actually take on and destroy the armoured emplacements with just the standard demolitions of the day. A stick grenade would scarcely scratch the concrete of a Maastricht 1 or a Coupole 120.

Even as Student stepped into Hitler's office on 27 October 1939, the Nazi leader had already been formulating a plan to overcome both these obstacles. Initial greetings over, Hitler took Student over to a map of Eben Emael and revealed that he wanted the Fallschirmjäger to take the fortress in the opening phase of the campaign in the West. Hitler also suggested that Student investigate DFS 230 gliders as the mode of deployment, inquiring whether the gliders could be landed directly atop the fortress roof.

The DFS 230 was a military transport glider designed in 1933 by one Dr Alexander Lippisch, although at first it was intended for meteorological use (Gukeison 1993: 23). By the mid-1930s, Germany was one of the world leaders in glider design and applications, not least because the Versailles Treaty's prohibition of a combat air force meant that for many years gliders were the main vehicles for training the aviators of the future Luftwaffe. Lippisch's design was picked up and developed for military purposes by the Deutsche Forschungsanstalt für Segelflug (German Research Institute for Sailplane Flight, or DFS) under lead designer Hans Jacobs. In 1938 Student acquired 12 of the gliders to form part of

APRIL 1940

Fallschirmjäger drop onto key targets during invasion of Denmark and Norway

the aviation section of the new 7. Flieger-Division. He demonstrated the applications of the gliders in the summer of that year, his division making a 12-glider practice assault at Jüterborg.

The DFS 230 was not necessarily an easy aircraft to fly into combat. It was cable-towed to the release point by a Ju 52 transport aircraft, a phase of the flight that rendered both aircraft vulnerable to enemy fighters and anti-aircraft fire. The glider had a limited range of control when gliding, and a precision landing depended largely on a well-judged approach. On touchdown the gliders were prone to skidding unpredictably on wet grass – something that made dawn or wet weather landings precarious – and a cautious enemy could protect itself against glider assault by embedding thick stakes in the ground in potential landing areas. That was the debit side of the equation, but the gliders also had many pluses. They could make almost silent approaches, thereby maximizing the element of surprise for an assault force. In the hands of a talented pilot, as subsequent tests proved, they could be placed easily within 100m of a given target, often as close as 20m, with a bit of luck and favourable weather. Most importantly, however, a single glider could deliver a nine-man airborne assault force with weapons at the ready, with a total payload of 2,000kg. Hitler asked Student – who was a capable glider pilot himself – to ponder whether a force of Fallschirmjäger could be deployed by glider right onto the grassy roof of Eben Emael itself.

Turning to the question of how the paras would tackle the armoured emplacements of the fortress, Hitler now revealed to Student the invention of a specialist range of demolitions ideal for the task. These were the *Hohlladungwaffen*, or hollow-charge weapons (this type of weapon is also known as a shaped charge). The foundations of the hollow charge were laid

in the early 1880s by German engineer Max von Föster (five years before US engineer Charles Monroe reported his own investigations into shaped charges), and went through several key stages of technical revision elsewhere to reach the devices used at Eben Emael. The basic principle of the hollow charge is that explosives are packed around an empty, conical metal liner, the broadest open end of the liner facing towards the target. When the explosive is detonated, the liner collapses under the pressure of the explosive, the metal turning into a single thin jet of metallic material travelling at

The DFS 230 glider was central to the German victory at Eben Emael. Not only did it enable pilots to land the assault teams within metres of their objectives, it also offered an almost-silent approach to the target and the capacity for carrying heavy assault gear. (Cody Images)

Paratroopers conduct a training exercise. This photo illustrates the typically light weaponry of the Fallschirmjäger, mainly focused around rifles and submachine guns with the MG 34 as a support weapon. The MG 34 here is mounted on a Lafette 34 tripod for sustained-fire roles. (Cody Images)

Charge Creuse 12.5Kgs
Hohlladung
12.5Kgs

Charge Explosive 3Kg
Geballteladung 3Kg

3kg

Charge Creuse 50Kgs
Hohlladung
50kg

Sprengbüchse 24 (1kg)
Charge Explosive 1kg

Demolition charges of the type used by the Fallschirmjäger at Eben Emael. The large 50kg two-piece shaped charge is on the left, next to the useful 12.5kg device. On the right are standard 3kg and 1kg explosives; the latter could be configured in multiple units to control the explosive force required. (Simon Dunstan)

hypersonic speed (up to 14km/sec) along the central axis of the liner cavity. This jet has exceptional properties of penetration against steel armour, in the region of 150–700 per cent of the jet's own diameter, so they also had equal applications to reinforced concrete emplacements. If the jet could penetrate to the interior of a casemate, the resulting 'spall' (fragments of concrete and metal) blown from the inside of the structure, plus the general blast effect, could injure or kill all of those inside. Even if the explosive did not manage to achieve full penetration, the shock waves alone were capable of producing a crippling spalling effect.

These weapons would be critical to the German success at Eben Emael. They came in two different explosive strengths. There was a 12.5kg device, and a far larger 50kg charge. The latter was so big that it came in two sections, each with its own carrying handle, the sections often being carried into action hung from poles nestling on the shoulders of two men. In addition to the shaped charges, the Germans carried a variety of conventional demolition charges, to destroy guns, blow doors and push through emplacement apertures.

FORCES ASSIGNED TO EBEN EMAEL AREA

Unit	Commander	Objective	Manpower
Sturmgruppe 'Stahl' ('Steel')	Oberleutnant Altmann	Bridge at Veldwezelt	1 officer, 91 men
Sturmgruppe 'Beton' ('Concrete')	Leutnant Schacht	Bridge at Vroenhoven	5 officers, 129 men
Sturmgruppe 'Eisen' ('Iron')	Leutnant Schächter	Bridge at Kanne	2 officers, 88 men
Sturmgruppe 'Granit' ('Granite')	Oberleutnant Witzig	Eben Emael	2 officers, 84 men

Having presented all his ideas, Hitler then sent Student away to consider the overall viability of the plan, and report back to him. Within 24 hours, Student returned to his leader and confirmed that the mission was sound in principle, and that he could start putting together a team to perform the raid. The mission to take Eben Emael was also given a codename – *Granit* ('Granite').

Training begins

Student's immediate priority was to put together the team that would take Eben Emael, plus the nearby bridges over the Albert Canal, which were also part of the Fallschirmjäger operation. This was created in the form of Sturmabteilung 'Koch' (Assault Detachment 'Koch'), named after its commander, Hauptmann Walter Koch. Koch took charge of a force of just under 440 men, drawn from I./FJR 1 and a platoon of Pioniere (combat engineers) from II./FJR 2.

Sturmabteilung 'Koch' would be subdivided as the weeks went on, with each Sturmgruppe of the assault force assigned a specific target for the forthcoming invasion. The organization broke down as follows.

A thoughtful reflection on this table indicates the scale of challenge the German paratroopers faced. All but one target was allocated fewer than 100 men. Eben Emael itself was scheduled to be taken by just a few dozen men led by the doubtless focused Oberleutnant Rudolf Witzig, the men chosen for their persuasive mix of combat skill and engineering know-how. The 24-year-old Witzig was certainly the right man for the job. Although ruthless and strict with his men, he was also a true combat leader, allowing his subordinates to exercise initiative in action and insisting on the realistic training that would pay dividends in action. Whatever his or his men's talents, however, the scale of the task made it clear that the outcome of the operations would be balanced on a knife edge.

Final authorization for the Eben Emael raid came within days of Student's meeting with Hitler, the para commander having reassured Hitler that a successful gliderborne assault was viable. Every scrap of intelligence was gathered for the operation. The commanders pored over aerial photographs and map work. They interviewed engineers and builders who had been connected with the construction of Eben Emael during the 1930s. They also oversaw the construction of scale models used for planning purposes. Note that not all of the intelligence gleaned during this early planning phase was rock solid – during the final planning for the raid, individual assault teams were designated to attack two of the false cupolas at Eben Emael.

Now training began in earnest. There was much to do. Not only did Koch have to familiarize his men with assaulting every aspect of their objectives, and plan for every permutation of disaster, he also had to give them training in use of the new explosives and bring 42 glider pilots of 17./KGrzbV 5 (17. Staffel, Kampfgruppe zur besonderen Verwendung 5, or '17 Squadron, Battle Group for Special Disposal 5') to the peak of their skill.

This latter point was crucial. Everything hung on the gliders deploying accurately to within metres of their intended targets. The further the distance

GERMAN FALLSCHIRMJÄGER AND BELGIAN INFANTRYMAN, 1940

The Fallschirmjäger shown here (**1**) was issued with uniform and kit that was cutting edge in the spring of 1940. He is wearing a Luftwaffe jump smock over his uniform, with his web equipment supporting magazine pouches for his MP 40 submachine gun and a pistol holster containing a Luger Pistole 08. A Model 24 *Stielhandgranate* grenade is held in the pocket of his jump smock, and the helmet is the cut-down para type. Around him is the weaponry of the Eben Emael raid: the Kar 98k carbine (**2**); the Flammenwerfer 35 flamethrower (**3**); the Hohlladung 50kg shaped charge (**4**); H12 12.5kg shaped charge (**5**); the standard 3kg assault charge (**6**); and 1kg assault charge (**7**). The bandolier (**8**) was for clips of 7.92mm carbine ammunition, and next to this is the standard-issue gravity knife (**9**) issued to all German paras. The paratrooper's opponent here is a Belgian infantryman (**10**), kitted out in a rather archaic uniform, including the 1915 model French *Adrian* steel helmet, here emblazoned with the Belgian lion. He is carrying a carbine version of the 7.65mm M1889 rifle, the shorter weapon often being issued to fortress troops. For heavier firepower he would rely on the FN 1930 Mle D (**11**), a Belgian variant of the US Browning Automatic Rifle (BAR) issued in 7.65×53mm Belgian Mauser.

the paras had to cross to their assault objectives, the greater the chance that they would succumb to defensive fire from the Belgian bunkers and troop positions. In addition, the Belgian forces in the area were expected to launch brisk counter-attacks once they became aware of the attack taking place; the Fallschirmjäger therefore had to have completed their initial missions at great speed, so they could take up defensive positions to meet the emerging threat.

In total, 42 gliders were allocated to the operation, each glider paired with a dedicated Ju 52 tow aircraft. During simulated landing trials for the Eben Emael attack, problems soon emerged. Even without the challenges of 42 pairs of gliders and tow aircraft flying in formation at night, putting 11 of those gliders down on the Eben Emael roof with the requisite precision was proving taxing. Skid landing often resulted in the gliders sliding way past their objectives, but the problem was partially solved by installing in each glider a wooden drag brake, essentially a wooden framework that pushed into the ground on landing, bringing the glider to a reasonably rapid halt. Witzig also scoured the Luftwaffe for the very best glider pilots available, including pre-war flying competition winners. Gukeison also notes that 'Oberleutnant Witzig took glider training one step further and incorporated the pilots into the assault sections. They were soon capable of employing every weapon in the platoon' (Gukeison 1993: 29). The investment in new technologies and skilled personnel paid off – soon the glider pilots were demonstrating the landing requirements demanded for the attack on Eben Emael, bringing their gliders to a halt within 10m of their training objectives.

For the assault troops themselves, the training was equally taxing. The men of Sturmabteilung 'Witzig' were flown out to various fortification sites in German-occupied Poland and Czechoslovakia, where they practised assaulting casemates and bunkers of a similar type to those they would face at Eben Emael. Physical training was constant and unforgiving; the men had to be able to run long distances in full battle gear, and carrying the extra weight of demolition charges, flamethrowers and other equipment. Each soldier received additional dedicated demolitions training, until he became an expert in destroying every conceivable type of fortress structure, from gun barrels to bunkers.

Secrecy was also of the utmost priority. Even though the paras weren't fully apprised of their target until a few hours before their mission, they had to keep silent about every aspect of their training and preparation. When going out in local towns and villages, they had their uniforms stripped of insignia and any identifying marks. They were forbidden from talking to locals, even signing a confidentiality clause that stated 'I am aware that I shall risk sentence of death should I, by intent or carelessness, make known to another person by spoken word or illustration anything concerning the base at which I am serving'. This was no idle threat – two Fallschirmjäger were indeed tried and executed for being loose with their tongues, even though they were only talking to members of another German unit (Dunstan 2005: 37). One unit was transferred from their base

An early-morning photograph taken on 10 May 1940 shows German paratroopers deploying over the Albert Canal. Air-dropped troops provided reinforcements to the glider-deployed soldiers attempting to capture the canal's key bridges. (Cody Images)

after some of its men bumped into a couple of girls whom they knew. Gliders were kept dismantled when not in use and transferred between positions in furniture vans. Furthermore, the German soldiers were not actually introduced to the hollow-charge demolitions devices until they were finally equipped for the raid; Hitler wanted to keep these new weapons to himself as much as he did the raid.

In terms of the actual plan itself, the broadest goals for the Eben Emael strike were as follows (see Gukeison 1993: 26 and Dunstan 2005: 38). The first objective was to take out the anti-aircraft positions and the machine-gun emplacements (Mi-Nord and Mi-Sud). These positions, with their close-range firepower, were actually ones that could threaten the successful deployment of the entire force, so they had to be knocked out in short order. The second objective was to knock out the guns oriented towards the bridges of Veldwezelt, Kanne and Vroenhoven, to enable the other Fallschirmjäger teams to secure these objectives and to prevent the artillery itself from destroying the bridges before German armour and troops could begin rolling across it. As a corollary of this objective, the paras also had to destroy the EBEN 2 and EBEN 3 observation domes, depriving the artillerymen of observation platforms. The third main objective was for the *Granit* team to knock out entrances and exits to the fortress. Note that this second objective implies a tactic of containment rather than outright destruction. It was acknowledged that a small group of Fallschirmjäger was simply not capable of wiping out a massive concrete fortress and killing all of its garrison. What it could do, however, was trap the garrison beneath ground, keeping it under control until general advances in the German campaign in Belgium obliged a surrender. About 40 minutes after the attack on Eben Emael began, the gliderborne assault on the three bridges would be launched by small teams. They would land as near to each bridge as possible, attack swiftly to neutralize the defenders and prevent any action to demolish the bridges.

The operation against Eben Emael and the nearby bridges would be launched around 0300hrs, with 42 glider/Ju 52 combinations taking off from the airfields of Köln-Butzweilerhof (ten gliders) and Köln-Ostheim. The two sets of aircraft would then rally around Efferen before being guided on a flight path – various forms of illumination, such as searchlights and bonfires, would mark the route – just north of Aachen, before the final run in to Eben Emael and the bridge targets. The gliders would be released approximately 27km from the targets, taking 12–14 silent and tense minutes to complete the journey. Total flight time would be roughly 50 minutes. (Note that Belgian time was one hour behind the time in Germany.)

Sturmgruppe 'Granit' was divided up into rigid areas of responsibility, the Trupp contained in each glider having responsibility for one primary objective, plus a secondary objective if the mission's development allowed. Each glider had to put its unit down within close proximity of its target, and all had to deploy in logical sequence on the roof of Eben Emael to prevent an air-control catastrophe in the early hours of the morning of 10 May.

Once on the ground, the Fallschirmjäger had to go swiftly to their objectives, destroy them with the hollow-charge weapons and other demolitions, and subdue the garrison inside. They had to move quickly, not only for the sake of the troops attacking the bridges, but also because it was expected that a Belgian counter-attack would probably be mounted within an hour of the landings. For this reason, special Luftwaffe ground-attack and supply units were also assigned a supporting role in the mission. A Luftwaffe air controller, Leutnant Egon Delica, was embedded with Sturmgruppe 'Granit' to co-ordinate Ju 87 strikes against Belgian forces moving against Eben Emael, plus supply drops to the German troops once they were dug in on the defence. Not that they were intended to hold on indefinitely. Generalmajor Johann Joachim Stever's 4. Panzer-Division was intended to cross the Albert Canal shortly after the bridges had been secured. One of its attached units, Pionier-Bataillon 51, would then head up to Eben Emael, helping the paratroopers quash whatever spark of resistance remained in the fortress, and oversee its eventual surrender.

From the initial planning phase of the Eben Emael raid to its final launch, the Fallschirmjäger had to endure numerous false starts and raised expectations. Then, on the evening of 9 May 1940, they received the codeword *Danzig*, the final authorization that the attack was about to begin. The Fallschirmjäger would now launch history's first gliderborne assault.

THE RAID

**2130hrs,
9 MAY 1940**

**Fallschirmjäger
units notified of
their objectives**

By May 1940, the Belgian garrison at Eben Emael was sick of hearing alerts. Every time the garrison was put on alert status – and it had happened on four occasions between November 1939 and April 1940 – leave was cancelled and duties increased, only for the men to be told again that the alarm was a false one. Morale in the garrison in general was at a very low ebb. There was virtually nothing for bored young men to do in the surrounding villages (Eben Emael and Wonck); the cities in the region were just too far away for easy access in the off-duty hours. Furthermore, physical conditions inside the fortress had been deteriorating for months. Damp pervaded the gloomy subterranean corridors, mixed with cement dust from flaking walls, together a perfect breeding ground for chest infections and other ailments.

There were also administrative and structural problems that would make a serious contribution to the fall of the fortress. Since Eben Emael had fallen under the command of 1er Corps headquarters in November 1939, its telecommunications connections with higher command were poor, mainly based upon wireless means and the civilian telephone network. (While the fort was under the authority of 3e Corps, it enjoyed the use of a dedicated military communications link.) The problem was exacerbated by a general lack of trained signallers in the fort in May 1940. To make matters worse, the individual gun emplacements had different command relationships to surrounding infantry and field artillery units. For example, Coupole 120 was 'controlled by Est d'A/CA du I.C.A; Coupole Nord and Sud by 7e Division d'Infanterie; Maastricht 1 and 2 by 18e Régiment d'Infanterie d'Ligne; Visé 1 by 2e Grenadiers Régiment; and Visé 2 by Sectuer Meuse-Aval' (Dunstan 2005: 40). The decision-making process regarding the demolition orders for the individual bridges was similarly fragmented, and the whole mess was given a further twist by the language issues of a mixed French- and Flemish-speaking garrison.

At 0030hrs on 10 May 1940, the fort authorities received another alert, the facts of which had been bubbling up through the Belgian high command

The two-storey Canal Nord bunker, set into the side of the Caster cutting, was armed with a 60mm anti-tank gun and three machine guns. Fallschirmjäger attempted, unsuccessfully, to destroy the bunker by lowering down shaped charges on ropes from the heights above the position. (Ulrich Heifer)

for the last three hours. Jottrand summoned his staff, who set about trying to organize Eben Emael onto something like a war footing. They faced some immediate challenges. At the time of the alert, the breakdown of personnel at the fort was as follows:

Command/adminstrative staff: 211 men
1er Batterie: 271 men
2e Batterie: 507 men

In addition to these figures, some 230 men were at stand-by positions at Wonck, 4km away. All told, Jottrand had 989 men to call upon, significantly below the fortress's full complement. A pre-arranged alert signal, in the form of 20 blank rounds fired by Coupole Nord, was put into abeyance, for reasons that still aren't entirely clear. When, at 0230hrs, the instruction to fire the gun was finally given, a confused situation prevented the order being implemented. Jottrand, short of men, had taken away gun crews to help him empty the contents of, then demolish, two administrative buildings near Bloc 1. This activity was in fulfilment of standing orders, but it was a distraction from more important affairs. Some warning shots were fired

**0330hrs,
10 MAY 1940**

**Fallschirmjäger's
towed gliders
begin taking off**

from Coupole Sud at 0325hrs, but the requisite pattern of fire was interrupted when the camouflage netting around the gun barrel caught fire.

In short, the response at Eben Emael to the general alert sweeping across Belgium was little short of farcical, as hours were frittered away in unnecessary acts and an ineffective call to action. By 0330hrs, moreover, Jottrand was becoming aware that this time the alert was likely to be genuine – from 0307hrs he could hear increasingly heavy gunfire from the direction of Maastricht, about 4km (2½ miles) away.

On the way

In contrast to the blunders taking place across the Belgian border, in Germany the Fallschirmjäger were demonstrating the professionalism for which they would become rightly famous. During the evening of 9 May, the men were told to stand by ready to go into action the next day, although they still didn't know their precise objective. (Many would have doubtless worked it out by this point.) Oberjäger Peter Arendt, Trupp 3 leader, captured the moment:

> Having reported 'all correct' to Leutnant Witzig at 2100, I paraded my troop and addressed them as follows: 'Comrades, we will be going into action tomorrow morning. We have to prove that we haven't wasted our time and that we have learned everything we were supposed to learn.' Then I dismissed them, telling them to get some rest. Reveille next morning was at 0245 and we paraded in full kit ready to emplane at 0330. (Quoted in Kühn 1978: 33)

Only at 2130hrs were the objectives of the assault revealed to the paratroopers. They then retired to their rooms, made final preparations, and those of iron constitution managed to grab a bit of sleep. Meanwhile all the gliders and their transports were readied for action on the two airfields.

One of the generators at Eben Emael. The underground fortress had the means for self-sufficiency in terms of power and ventilation, but once the garrison was trapped beneath the surface by the German assault, atmospheric conditions quickly became intolerable. (B25es)

Only a few hours after retiring to their quarters, the Fallschirmjäger were roused into action, pulled all their gear together and headed out onto their respective airfields to board the assault gliders. The armada began taking off around 0330hrs (Belgian time), with all aircraft airborne by 0335hrs. Obergefreiter Wilhelm Alefs of Trupp 7 captured the moment of launch perfectly:

It was very black. I felt around and found the explosives and everything else as it should be and as I left it five hours earlier. I patted the pockets of my jacket to feel the grenades, then the ones above to see if my machine pistol ammunition was there, unconscious and reassuring gestures. I reached into the pocket of my inner jacket to feel the fuse and cord for the explosives. The glider began rocking as the pilots of the tow planes revved the engines whose roar was muffled to us in the now tightly closed glider. We didn't take off at once. There were many other planes and gliders to take off ahead of us, and it was those I could hear power up as they went down the runway. Suddenly a jerk on the glider forced me backwards. There was a jockeying and sloshing motion as the towrope tightened and swung the glider behind the straining plane ahead. Simultaneously, we all started that chant of the paratroopers – 'Rot Scheint die Sonne, fertig gemacht' ['Red shines the sun, be ready']. (Quoted in Dunstan 2005: 44)

The mission to take Eben Emael and the bridges of the Albert Canal was now under way, but there was an early mishap that threatened to shake the confidence of the fortress assault, as Trupp 3 commander Peter Arendt related:

We walked over to the gliders, climbed in, and at precisely 0430 the 11 aircraft tugs took off towing us up towards the morning sky.

Sometime [sic] later our aircraft and gliders rendezvoused with the 11 gliders of the 'Iron' section which had taken off from the Cologne-Butzweilerhof airfield. And it was then that an unforeseen and wholly unanticipated accident threatened the hitherto smooth running organization of the operation. Manoeuvring into a compact air formation the machine pulling the glider with Leutnant Witzig aboard flew across the path of one of the other aircraft, and Witzig's pilot had to bank sharply to avoid his tow rope getting entangled with that of the second glider. Unfortunately the extra stress occasioned by this evasive manoeuvre resulted in the tow rope snapping and Witzig's glider was no longer under tow. Turning back, the pilot was just able to get his glider back across the Rhine before landing. But the assault section had lost its commander. (Quoted in Kühn 1978: 33)

Witzig would later return to the battle, but for now the Eben Emael force had to continue on without its leader. Fortunately, both training and the German command structure meant that the raid could continue without a loss of direction. Yet the problems mounted as the flight continued. A misunderstanding over signalling procedures resulted in the Ju 52 pilot responsible for towing Trupp 2 ordering glider release too soon and at too low an altitude. At first the glider pilot, Unteroffizier Bredenbeck, resisted the order, but 'shake-off' manoeuvres by the Ju 52 eventually forced his compliance and the glider drifted down over German territory. So within minutes of taking off, the German forces was reduced to just 70 men.

Total flying time to target, including a 12–14-minute glider descent, was about 50 minutes. A tailwind pushed the aircraft to the release point too early, however, and the Ju 52 pilots were forced to make a circuit out over Dutch territory both to get back on schedule and to gain the correct altitude for release. The brief excursion over the Netherlands elicited some anti-aircraft fire, without loss, then the gliders of Sturmabteilung 'Koch' were finally released at around 0410hrs, with an intended landing time of 0425hrs.

The German gliders, unmarked to produce confusion amongst the defenders, eventually began to touch down upon the roof of Eben Emael. (Note that the assaults on the bridges are described separately, but went in almost simultaneously with the Eben Emael assault.) In the half-light of dawn, the Belgian soldiers atop the fort saw the gliders emerge through a light mist. At first there was little but confusion; one of the Belgian officers even thought that the aircraft were British reconnaissance planes. A few of the MICA guns eventually sprang into life, but by this point it was too late, as the German gliders were already beginning to touch down. (A total of six gliders were peppered by machine-gun fire, although no casualties were sustained.)

L. Meeson, the chaplain of Eben Emael, remembered the events of 9 May 1940 in his diary. As first-hand accounts from the actual attack are relatively few, it is worth quoting the passage in full, if only to show how ill-prepared the Belgian forces were to meet the airborne attack:

Thursday 9 May 1940. The news is good tonight – five-day leave passes have been reinstated. The troops are making plans. As for me, I have decided to take three days off between 20 and 23 of May... Around 9 o'clock, we go back to the fort. Not knowing what to do at the village many soldiers are returning as well. The news about the restoration of leave is spreading. Once again everything is going extremely well ... Half-past twelve at night. We were woken up by the sound of a bugle and pandemonium in the galleries. It's the alarm. Is it real this time or will it be another drill again? And what about our leave? The outcome of each alert has always been the cancellation of leave for an unspecified length of time... Everything is quiet. No sound or light from the village. As with every other alarm everything from the outside buildings has to be

Sidebar

0425hrs,
10 MAY 1940

Sturmgruppe 'Granit' begins to land on the roof of Eben Emael

Caption

German infantry and armour advance during the early stages of *Fall Gelb*. The Fallschirmjäger in Belgium had to secure key bridges and the fortress at Eben Emael to ensure the smooth advance of ground forces from the north-east. (Cody Images)

moved into the fort – officers' mess, records and files. The men are working willingly. Nobody is expecting a war. Some of them, thinking of their leave, are working reluctantly.

... I intend to go back when I am told that twenty gunshots will be fired from Coupole 120. This seems to be getting serious. Could this really mean war? The major has been told that the turret is not working. An act of sabotage? I believe that the shots will be fired from another cupola. At that time I reached my room inside the fort and couldn't hear the twenty shots being fired... Father Lamaye who did not leave comes to see me around four thirty – 'We are at war!' he says. 'German planes have landed on the fort. So it is real this time. I put my helmet on, take my gas mask and we go out into the passage... The men are bustling about everywhere. What is going on above us? I am going to the infirmary. Our three doctors are there, Commandant Willems and Lieutenants Dumay and Steegen. Doctor Steegen tells us that he has seen planes coming down onto the fort. The machines were flying silently, their engines stopped. Yet at that time we didn't know they were planes without engines – gliders! (Quoted in Dunstan 2005: 48)

Fallschirmjäger gather around a map placed on the wing of a Ju 52, studying their intended landing zones. Only in the immediate hours before the Eben Emael operation did the men of Sturmgruppe 'Granit' learn of their assault objective, although many must have suspected it would be Eben Emael. (Cody Images)

Further investigation after the raid revealed that during the first crucial minutes of the Eben Emael action, the wrong sort of alert was sounded, telling the troops that the fortress was facing attack from the surrounding countryside, not that the top of the fortress itself was compromised. All these failures would feed into a disaster for the Belgian troops that day.

The first glider to land was that of Trupp 5 headed by Erwin Haug, which had the MICA as its primary objective. The precision landing by pilot Unteroffizier Heiner Lange was performed with such aplomb that the wing of the glider actually smashed up one of the machine guns. Quickly the paratroopers disgorged from the glider, throwing grenades at the gun emplacements and firing with their small arms. Quickly, four Belgians in one position surrendered, while at another nearby position one Belgian soldier was killed and two wounded in this opening act of the attack.

Within minutes of the assault on the MICA positions, the rest of the gliders were down on the roof of Eben Emael and multiple positions assaults were under way. We will treat each position separately, but together they formed a dynamic attack pattern that threatened to overwhelm the defenders' responses.

A bunker burns during a German assault, possibly at Eben Emael. Although the German airborne troops did not have the resources to destroy Eben Emael comprehensively, they could trap the garrison within their ferro-concrete emplacements, and keep them there until reinforcements arrived. (Cody Images)

Coupole Nord

One of the first units to swing into action at Eben Emael was Trupp 8, which had Coupole Nord as its objective. The respective glider was skilfully flown in by Unteroffizier Hans Distelmeier, who landed his aircraft within 20m of the target. The men emerged from their glider and immediately began to be hit by machine-gun fire from the MICA hut, which Lieutenant Longdoz was defending with a small group of men and two machine guns. Subduing this position with Trupp 5, after Trupp 8 had taken Coupole Nord, cost the Germans one wounded and two dead, the first German casualties of the battle.

The Fallschirmjäger were quickly into action with their new demolition charges. A 50kg charge was placed atop the cupola of Coupole Nord, while another 12.5kg charge was set against the door. The initial effects of their explosion were mixed – the 50kg charge didn't manage to penetrate the structure, but the cupola door and its surrounding concrete structure collapsed. At the time when the 50kg charge went off, the Belgian occupants inside, commanded by Maréchal des logis Joiris, were hauling 75mm canister ammunition up via the staircase to the cupola, the mechanical hoists having failed (one of several mechanical breakdowns that day, prompting some to speculate later about the possibilities of sabotage). The 12.5kg detonation had far more serious human effects, killing one man and wounding four others. The Germans outside then detonated another 50kg charge against the cupola, and although the external damage was disappointing for the attackers, the explosions of this charge nevertheless penetrated the cupola and rendered the guns inoperable, as well as preventing the cupola from turning. Coupole Nord was now effectively out of action, and the surviving occupants simply sealed up the position and at 0545hrs retreated back into the bowels of the fortification. Trupp 8 leader Otto Unger, one of the men who was at the head of the attack on Coupole Nord, was among the German dead sustained suppressing the Belgian troops fighting from the MICA hut.

Even as the attack on Coupole Nord was going in, other paras were wasting their efforts destroying the false cupolas at the northern end of the fortress. Trupp 7, led by Fritz Heinemann, was the first to touch down in the vicinity of these objectives. The landing was not a good one – the glider came down too heavily and two men were injured in the process. It was quickly discovered that the objectives were nothing more than fake sheet-steel positions, although they were still destroyed with demolition charges, to make it clear that these weren't operational positions. Trupp 6 flew in to assist in the assault, and also made a difficult landing; this time the glider was caught up in barbed-wire barriers and it took some minutes for the soldiers inside to break free from the glider. When they did so, they found that their comrades in Trupp 7 had already taken the two false cupolas out of the equation. The options for the two units contributing further to the action at Eben Emael were limited because an earth rampart running between Mi-Sud and Mi-Nord formed a barrier between them and the other assault teams further south. Instead, the two groups of doubtless disgruntled soldiers adopted defensive positions facing the river Geer.

Mi-Sud and Mi-Nord

As already discussed, Mi-Sud and Mi-Nord were not the most powerful of the emplacements within Eben Emael, but their machine-gun armament could do serious damage to the paras assaulting within the fortress confines. Yet in both cases the fears of the Germans about these positions were unfounded. At Mi-Sud, the glider of Trupp 9 went in as planned and landed in close proximity to the objective. The paras disembarked and proceeded to cut through the barbed-wire entanglements that led up to their objective. Although there was small-arms fire coming from other sectors of Eben Emael, the armoured shutters of Mi-Sud were actually closed, and no fire came from the position (the Belgian occupants had fled). This fact enabled the paras to close up to Mi-Sud and, after some practical difficulties, emplace a 50kg charge to a machine-gun embrasure, which was obliterated in the subsequent blast. Mi-Sud consequently fell without German bloodshed or risk.

A similar story played out at Mi-Nord. This position was the responsibility of Trupp 4, headed by Oberfeldwebel Wenzel. The landing was a volatile one, and the glider ended up some 80m away from its objective. As the German paratroopers emerged from the glider they faced very heavy machine-gun fire from the position, but as they closed the distance the intensity of fire diminished significantly and then went completely silent. By the time the soldiers arrived at the emplacement, the armoured shutters had come up. As a first action, Wenzel and two others climbed up onto the top of the position and detonated a 1kg explosive charge in the EBEN 2 armoured observation dome. One man was injured, but the Belgian machine-gun fire started up again in response. Wenzel decided to upgrade the force options. He put in place a 50kg hollow charge atop EBEN 2, and set the fuse running. When the charge went off, the explosive jet of molten metal did not penetrate the armoured carapace, but the blast overpressure killed two of the occupants and wounded several others, and it jammed EBEN 2 so that it could no longer revolve. Another of the fortress's eyes was blinded.

TAKING EBEN EMAEL – THE PLAN

10 MAY 1940

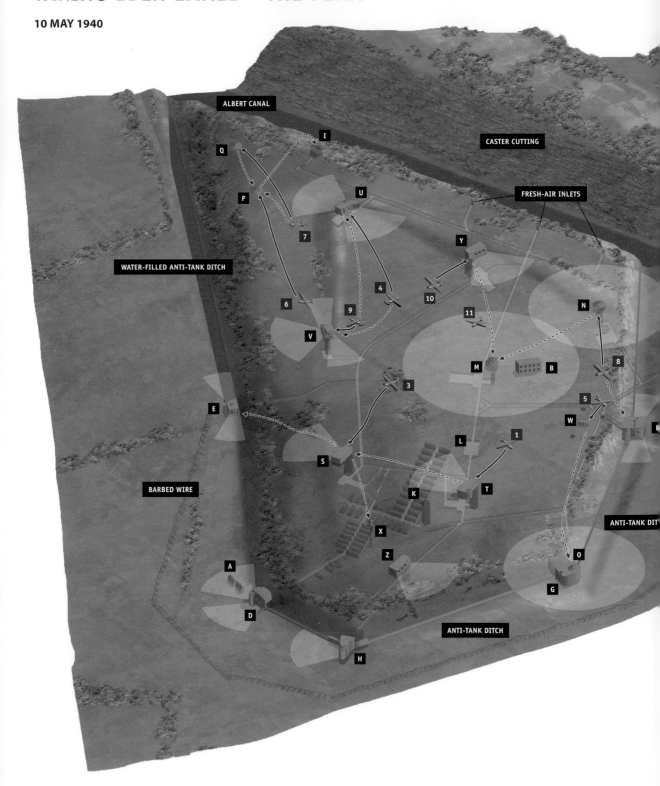

ALBERT CANAL

CASTER CUTTING

FRESH-AIR INLETS

WATER-FILLED ANTI-TANK DITCH

BARBED WIRE

ANTI-TANK DIT

ANTI-TANK DITCH

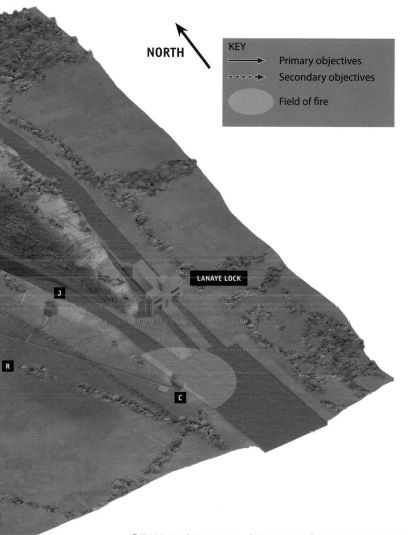

NORTH

KEY

→ Primary objectives

----→ Secondary objectives

Field of fire

LANAYE LOCK

J

R

C

STRUCTURES A-Z

A. Administrative buildings

B. Baraque Graindorge

C. Bloc 01 and EBEN 1 (Obj. 34)

D. Bloc 1 (Obj. 3)

E. Bloc 2 (Obj. 4)

F. Bloc 4 (Obj. 30)

G. Bloc 5 (Obj. 22)

H. Bloc 6 (Obj. 6)

I. Canal Nord (Obj. 17)

J. Canal Sud (Obj. 38)

K. Caserne souterraine

L. Command post

M. Coupole 120 (Obj. 24)

N. Coupole Nord (Obj. 31)

O. Coupole Sud (Obj. 23)

P. False cupola (Obj. 14)

Q. False cupola (Obj. 16)

R. False cupola (Obj. 32)

S. Maastricht 1 (Obj. 12)

T. Maastricht 2 and EBEN 3 (Obj. 18)

U. Mi-Nord and EBEN 2 (Obj. 19)

V. Mi-Sud (Obj. 13)

W. MICA anti-aircraft position (Obj. 29)

X. Ventilation shaft

Y. Visé 1 (Obj. 26)

Z. Visé 2 (Obj. 9)

STURMGRUPPE 'GRANIT' OBJECTIVES BY TRUPP 1-11

Trupp	Trupp leader	Primary objective(s)	Secondary objective(s)
1. Trupp 1	Feldwebel Hans Niedermeier	Maastricht 2 and EBEN 3	Maastricht 1
2. Trupp 2 (flight aborted)	Oberjäger Max Maier	Coupole 120	MICA anti-aircraft position; Visé 1
3. Trupp 3	Oberjäger Peter Arendt	Maastricht 1	Bloc 2; ventilation shaft
4. Trupp 4	Oberfeldwebel Helmut Wenzel	Mi-Nord and EBEN 2	Mi-Sud
5. Trupp 5	Feldwebel Erwin Haug	MICA anti-aircraft position	Coupole Sud
6. Trupp 6	Oberjäger Siegfried Harlos	False cupola (Obj. 14)	Canal Nord
7. Trupp 7	Oberjäger Fritz Heinemann	False cupola (Obj. 16)	False cupola (Obj. 14)
8. Trupp 8	Oberjäger Otto Unger	Coupole Nord	Bloc 4; Coupole 120
9. Trupp 9	Oberjäger Ewald Neuhaus	Mi-Sud	Mi-Nord and EBEN 2
10. Trupp 10	Oberjäger Willi Hübel	Visé 1	Coupole 120
11. Trupp 11	Oberjäger Fritz Schwarz	Reserve	Reserve

German troops contemplate a demolished bridge over the river Maas at Maastricht. Dutch and Belgian efforts to stop the German advance by demolishing bridges failed, and the Fallschirmjäger's capture of bridges over the Meuse aided the German Army's push towards northern France. (Cody Images)

The paras followed up this explosive assault with more demolition and shaped charges, with horrible effects on those inside the position. Eventually the defenders recognized the impossibility of their situation, and shrank down inside the fortress, sealing off the corridor behind them.

Maastricht 1 and Maastricht 2

The attackers destined to assault Maastricht 1 and 2 were faced with emplacements that, at first glance, were well beyond the concrete-cracking powers of just a handful of men. The Maastricht 1 team was headed by Oberjäger Arendt, who was accompanied by the six others who made up Trupp 3. Inside the position were 7–10 Belgian defenders, led by Maréchal des logis Gigon. Trupp 3's glider had a somewhat difficult approach to Eben Emael, as it was forced to make three circuits before finally touching down. By the time the aircraft stopped sliding across the wet fortress grass, however, the men were within 25m of their intended objective.

Arendt and his men were soon swarming around the position, trying to find the best place to position their charges to blow their way inside. At first, the men attempted to emplace one of the 50kg charges against the surface of the position, but this proved to be impossible. (Shaped charges need to be positioned flat against the plane of their target, otherwise the excessive gap between charge and surface dissipates the penetrative force of the explosion.) As a second option the soldiers then successfully positioned a 12.5kg charge into the embrasure of the left-hand 75mm gun. The fuse was triggered and the men retreated to a safe distance. An enormous explosion blew out the 75mm gun barrel and punched a wide black hole in the concrete, from which smoke poured.

Inside Maastricht 1 there was chaos and carnage. The emplacement was filled with choking cordite smoke, and fire began to lick around the ammunition. One man had been killed and several others wounded,

including Gigon. As the walking survivors attempted to get the injured men down below into the safety of the fort, outside Arendt and his men were following up on their explosive attack. Arendt himself ran up to the hole in the emplacement, threw two hand grenades inside and emptied a burst of submachine-gun fire into the interior, from which he could hear the groans of the wounded. He then pushed his way in, groping around in the smoky darkness. The rest of the German squad soon joined him, especially as shells from Coupole Sud began at this point to land around Maastricht 1. Three Belgian soldiers were captured, and Arendt took one of them with him as he began to explore deeper into the fortress depths. He dropped a 2kg demolition charge down an ammunition elevator shaft, then descended a long flight of stairs. James E. Mrazek, who wrote one of the definitive accounts of the Eben Emael battle in 1970 (based heavily upon interviews with veterans of the raid), recounts how even the stairs presented challenges to the German attackers:

> He [Arendt] counted 118 stairs. In three places the treads were missing. The Germans concluded that the Belgians had designed the stairs so that certain treads could be quickly removed. An enemy, unaware treads were missing would likely fall through the opening and be injured or killed in the drop to the concrete floor storeys below. This would slow, if not dissuade, any enemy from pursuing the defenders down the stairwells and into the interior of the fort. (Mrazek 1972: 95)

Inside the triple 75mm casemates. The walls of these emplacements were 2.75m thick, and two of them were also built into the earth for added protection.(Illustration by Hugh Johnson, © Osprey Publishing)

A new age of warfare. German paratroopers spill out over Dutch territory on 10 May 1940. As well as the action at Eben Emael, the Fallschirmjäger conducted equally high-risk operations over key targets in the Netherlands, securing several vital airfields. (Cody Images)

Mrazek goes on to recount how Arendt made it successfully to the bottom of the stairs, without slipping to his doom, whereupon he found the way deeper into the heart of the fortress blocked by the combined door, beam and sandbag blockade. Therefore he returned to the casemate above ready to fight against any potential Belgian counter-attack. At least Maastricht 1 was firmly in German hands now.

Maastricht 2 (and EBEN 3) was the focus of Hans Niedermeier's Trupp 1, which also included Egon Delica, the Luftwaffe air liaison officer. Their landing was a far rougher affair than that experienced by their Trupp 8 comrades. The glider hit the ground in a hurry, its incoming flight disrupted by Belgian anti-aircraft fire. As it raced across the grass the skid of the glider dug in and the whole aircraft spun around, cracking one of the wing spars and causing other damage. None of the occupants were hurt, however, and they were quickly out of the glider and storming towards their objective.

On reaching Maastricht 2, Niedermeier and Gefreiter Richard Drucks pulled themselves up onto the EBEN 3 armoured observation dome and put in place a 50kg shaped charge (each man had been carrying half the charge). Once the charge was in place, exactly over the centre of the dome, the fuse was set and the men jumped down to take cover from the detonation. The resulting blast killed the two unfortunate occupants of the dome. As with Maastricht 1, the assault team then placed a 12.5kg charge under the left-hand 75mm gun, which when it exploded destroyed the gun and killed two more men, as well as seriously wounding another.

In a flash Niedermeier and his men were inside the emplacement, wearing gasmasks in the smoke-filled interior. They dropped 3kg explosive charges down the ammunition shaft leading up to the emplacement, but were unable to go much further because of the internal barriers erected by the Belgians. At least part of the defenders' response plan was working.

Consolidating the attack

Only 20 minutes into the Eben Emael action, an extraordinary German victory was in the making. Although there were still large numbers of Belgian defenders below ground, and despite the mounting probability of a major Belgian counter-attack, for the time being Sturmgruppe 'Granit' was in effective control of the surface of Eben Emael fortress. It had achieved this despite being deprived of two gliders on the way in, and of its overall commander. Moreover, the level of casualties had been remarkably light so far – two dead and 12 wounded. Five of the fort's major gun emplacements, plus its anti-aircraft battery, had been destroyed. The bridges over the Albert Canal were safe from the fort's long-range gunnery. The primary objective for the Germans now was to keep the Belgians trapped underground.

Although the Germans were in the ascendant, much needed to be done for them to stay in that position. The fortress's perimeter defences were still operational, and at 0450hrs the first of the day's Luftwaffe air support arrived, in the form of Ju 87 Stuka dive-bombers that started to attack the positions around the edge of Eben Emael, and also gave Coupole Sud a pounding, without putting it out of action. Several key emplacements had also managed so far to avoid destruction. These included Visé 1 and Visé 2, Coupole Sud and the mighty Coupole 120.

In the absence of Witzig, the effective leader of the paras was now Oberfeldwebel Wenzel; Leutnant Delica was better suited to his role of air liaison officer, rather than taking control of an infantry force. Reinforcements had just flown in in the form of the Trupp 10 reserve, providing a small boost in manpower. They also brought with them a radio, and Wenzel was able to make contact with Koch back at headquarters, transmitting the blunt message: 'Target reached. Everything in order.' Wenzel also radioed for resupply of ammunition. This came shortly afterwards, when two He 111 bombers flew low over the fortress and dropped two containers full of additional ammunition.

The containers lay in open ground, but retrieving them was now no simple matter. By this point all of Belgium's armed forces were on a war footing, and Eben Emael was beginning to receive increasingly heavy artillery fire from nearby fortifications. In total, some 2,200 shells would be fired into Eben Emael, but thankfully for the Germans they had ready-made armoured emplacements into which they could retreat when things became too hot for them to be outside. In the case of the air-dropped containers, however, Wenzel found a solution in sending Belgian prisoners to collect the containers, which they did.

One of Wenzel's first command decisions, from his new headquarters inside Mi-Nord, was to take the fight to Visé 1, which was by this time firing out from the fort. A small force of paras was soon surrounding and atop the position, and a 12.5kg hollow charge wrecked the gun that had been firing. The explosion forced the occupants of the emplacement down below, and although some later returned to the surface to fire the occasional shell from the other guns, Visé 1 was essentially out of commission. Its observation cupola was also destroyed by the German team.

Assault on Maastricht 2 (overleaf)

Fallschirmjäger of Hans Niedermeier's Trupp 1 take cover against the earthen bank of the Maastricht 2 emplacement as a 12.5kg shaped charge detonates beneath a 75mm gun embrasure. The EBEN 3 armoured observation dome atop the emplacement had already been damaged by a 50kg shaped charge, and the explosion of the smaller demolition device wrecked a gun and killed two men inside, and wounded a third. The assault team then moved into the emplacement and dropped 3kg charges down the position's ammunition shaft. The 75mm quick-firing guns of positions such as Maastricht 2 could deliver heavy fire on the bridges at Kanne, Vroenhoven and Veldwezelt, and so had to be taken out as quickly as possible by the assault paratroopers. The 12.5kg charge proved particularly well suited to demolishing gun apertures and punching holes through the ferro-concrete structures.

A view of Coupole 120 and (in the background) Maastricht 2. This perspective gives a sense of the open areas around the surface of Eben Emael, which provided the Fallschirmjäger with landing zones for the DFS 230 gliders. If these surfaces had been fitted with anti-glider obstacles, the Eben Emael assault would have been a disaster. (Scargill)

Now it was the turn of Coupole Sud to face the attention of the Fallschirmjäger. Trupp 5 took charge of this action at 0530hrs, and five minutes later they detonated a 50kg charge on the position (the cupola was retracted at this point). The damage caused by the explosion convinced the Germans that they had managed to knock Coupole Sud out, but in fact the damage was limited, and it was subsequently repaired by the resilient gun crew inside. It was not the first time that the 50kg charges had let the paras down that day, unlike the more versatile 12.5kg charge that opened up many of the emplacements.

Coupole 120, meanwhile, sat brooding and silent. Trupp 2 was meant to have knocked out this position by now, but even though the unit hadn't in fact made it to the fortress, the remaining German troops believed that it had been silenced by one of the assault groups. In fact, the emplacement was occupied by its gun crew, commanded by Maréchal des logis Cremers, who was attempting to bring the gun to life. This had serious implications for the overall mission of Sturmgruppe 'Granit', as Coupole 120 was the only gun position that still had the capacity to threaten the bridges over the Albert Canal. Cremers spotted German troops milling around the cupola, and responded by firing his rifle at them, aiming through the aperture meant for the cupola's telescopic sight. His shots wounded a German glider pilot and a Belgian prisoner, but they also had the effect of alerting the Germans to the fact that the emplacement was still active.

The Fallschirmjäger reacted quickly. They pushed 1kg demolition charges directly into the 120mm barrels, and when these exploded they vented the blast through the guns' open breeches into the interior of the emplacement. The lights in the cupola went out, and Cremers and his men retreated down into the bowels of the fortress.

The saga of Coupole 120 was, however, far from over. Wenzel wanted to ensure that it was emphatically out of commission, so around 0645hrs the emplacement was attacked with a 50kg shaped charge, which served to damage the two guns. The Belgian gun crew nevertheless showed some remarkable persistence, returning to the position where they managed to repair one of the guns and get it ready for action. Not for the first time that day, the Belgian defenders were let down by the inefficiencies of the higher

command. Cremers now had ample targets formed by the build-up of German forces on the eastern side of the Meuse, as key bridges over the river had been blown, meaning that the Germans were forced to make improvised crossings and repairs. Yet even though communications were established between Cremers and headquarters, he never received permission to open fire.

A golden opportunity to affect the expansion of the German operations was therefore lost. Instead the paras continued to try to knock out the silent emplacement. Around 0900hrs, the soldiers would stuff multiple explosive charges, including heavier 3kg varieties, down the barrels of the guns. The blasts caused serious damage to both the emplacement and the guns; a later actual attempt to fire one of the guns resulted in nothing more than a split barrel. Ironically, around 1000hrs the cupola finally received fire orders, by which time Cremers and his men had completely abandoned their now-destroyed emplacement.

Although the Germans were skilfully consolidating their hold over the interior positions of the fortress at Eben Emael, those on the peripheries largely remained in Belgian hands. Indeed Bloc 1 became the launch point for some of the earliest Belgian counter-attacks of the day – not that these gave the Germans much cause for concern. The first of the attacks, moving towards Maastricht 1, consisted of only 14 men led by Lieutenant DeSloovere, none of them armed with automatic weapons. Their progress was abruptly stopped when the observation dome of nearby Bloc 2 disintegrated under the blast of a 50kg demolition charge, courtesy of the soldiers of Trupp 3. (One Belgian observer was killed in the blast.) Another minor counter-attack at 0800hrs did little other than anger Jottrand, who was becoming increasingly disaffected with the efforts of the men under his command.

Bloc 2 at Eben Emael. The attacking German forces eventually suppressed this position with a 50kg shaped charge placed on the position's observation dome, killing the occupant of the dome. (Scargill)

**0830hrs,
10 MAY 1940**

**Witzig arrives to
take command of
Sturmgruppe
'Granit'**

While events were playing out at Coupole 120 and around Bloc 1, Wenzel's temporary period in command came to an end with, for the Germans, a welcome arrival, as recounted by para Kurt Engelmann:

> It was around 0830hrs when a lone glider flew over the fort and landed not very far away from the northern rampart. In it was Oberleutnant Witzig and Trupp 11, who had been forced to land in a meadow beside the Rhine when the tow rope broke shortly after take-off. In a relatively short time, Witzig was able to organize a replacement Ju 52 tow aircraft, which was able to land on the meadow and take-off again with the DFS 230 of Trupp 11. Witzig was quickly briefed by Fw Wenzel and he assumed command of the assault group. (Quoted in Dunstan 2005: 55)

Witzig's arrival was welcomed by the Fallschirmjäger of Sturmgruppe 'Granit'. Yet Witzig, while appreciative of their initial enthusiasm, was in a businesslike mood, and asked for a quick update on the situation and the outstanding tasks at hand. He quickly assigned tasks for the destruction of Coupole 120 (described above) but his key order was 'to blow in the fortified entrances and press the attack into the depths of the fortress, holding all captured positions until relief arrived' (Witzig 1966: 109). Even though the effective part of Witzig's command now consisted of just 60 men, it was time to finish off Eben Emael.

The bridges

The Fallschirmjäger at Eben Emael were not the only German paras fighting hard during the early hours of 10 May 1940. Strategically integrated with the taking of the Belgian fortress was the capture of the three critical bridges over the Albert Canal at Veldwezelt, Vroenhoven and Kanne. The importance of these operations was sharpened by the fact that an Abwehr assault team responsible for capturing road bridges over the Meuse was unsuccessful

Coupole 120 (foreground) sat in the centre of Fort Eben Emael and contained the fortress's heaviest weaponry – two 120mm guns. The armoured cupola alone weighed some 230 tonnes. Coupole Nord can be seen in the background, to the right. (Wasily)

in preventing the Dutch defenders from blowing the bridges up, meaning that the flow of German forces into the West was now disrupted. It was also possible that the essential reinforcements for Eben Emael would be delayed, leaving the Fallschirmjäger out on their own for longer.

Individual assault teams were allocated to each of the bridges. Sturmgruppe 'Stahl' ('Steel'), commanded by Oberleutnant Gustav Altmann, was headed for the bridge at Veldwezelt, and consisted of nine gliders and 92 men. Sturmgruppe 'Eisen' ('Iron'), led by Leutnant Martin Schächter, was responsible for the bridge at Kanne, and had 90 men in ten gliders. Finally, Sturmgruppe 'Beton' ('Concrete') was the largest of the bridge-assault teams, involving 11 gliders and 134 men, commanded by Leutnant Gerhard Schacht.

Holes created by German shaped charges in the EBEN 3 observation dome atop Maastricht 2. The cutting power of the new weapons was immense, bu in many cases the explosive jet created by the charges still failed to penetrate through to the interior of the Belgian positions. (Wasily)

As with the fortress assault, the Belgian forces holding the bridges suffered from procedural complexities that would dog the defence of their positions. The bridges at Veldwezelt and Vroenhoven, for example, were commanded by Capitaine-commandant Giedelo stationed some distance away at Lanaken, Belgium, rather than having an on-site or at least proximate commander. Kanne, by contrast, was the responsibility of Jottrand at Eben Emael. All bridges were wired with demolition charges, and if the spans were brought down before the German forces had a chance to cross, the consequences for the German advance could be severe. Yet if the communications between the bridges and higher headquarters were disrupted, as they were during the early hours of the German campaign in the West, then the Fallschirmjäger had a window of opportunity to exploit.

The assault gliders began to touch down around the bridges from 0415hrs, the Belgian troops at the objectives being as stunned as their comrades at Eben Emael by this sudden aerial threat. The response of the men at Kanne, the nearest bridge to the fortress, was the most effective of the day, aided by its more streamlined command structure direct to Jottrand. The glider landings around the bridge were erratic. One glider, that of Trupp 1, didn't make it at all – it was released too early and landed too far away from its objective. The Trupp 3 glider was struck by anti-aircraft fire on its approach, catching fire and taking casualties. The other gliders, navigation hampered by early-morning mist, landed in scattered positions around the bridge, and so weren't able to assault in a co-ordinated fashion. Those who did approach the bridge were faced with heavy fire from the various bunkers and troop positions dotted around the banks of the canal, armed with 47mm anti-tank guns and machine guns. Then the worst possible outcome for the Germans occurred. Seeing that they were under attack, the occupants of Bloc 0

The Bloc 0 position overlooking the Kanne bridge over the Albert Canal. The bridge lies in the water – it was successfully demolished before Sturmgruppe 'Eisen' was able to capture it, although German infantry was still able to move across the bridge's exposed girders. (National Archives and Records Administration)

overlooking the bridge briskly contacted Jottrand at Eben Emael, who ordered the immediate destruction of the bridge. The charges were then detonated, and the Fallschirmjäger watched in despair as the bridge slumped into the river. The bridge could still be crossed, albeit carefully, by soldiers on foot, as enough of the structure remained above water for the girders to act as walkways.

It was just the beginning of the ordeal for the paras at Kanne bridge. The small group of men dug in on the west bank of the canal and began to exchange fire with the Belgian troops, who launched a series of counter-attacks that continued throughout the day until early evening. Casualties mounted among the Germans – by 1200hrs they had suffered four dead and six seriously wounded. Reinforcements in the form of Infanterie-Regiment 151 reached them at 2230hrs, but by the time they were relieved from the line around daybreak on the 11th the paras had suffered 22 dead and 26 wounded, plus one missing in action. Belgian casualties were far heavier: 150 dead and nearly 300 taken prisoner. One interesting point to note, illustrative of the tenacity of the Fallschirmjäger, was that while the battle was taking place, Trupp 2 of Sturmgruppe 'Granit' arrived at the bridge, its members having made their way across land following their impromptu glider release. To get to this point, the troop leader, Oberjäger Maier, requisitioned two staff cars from an engineer unit near Düren, and the paras drove through the confusion of Belgium in the early hours of the invasion, threatened not only by Belgian forces but also by Luftwaffe ground-attack aircraft, who might confuse the vehicles (which were well ahead of the main German advance) with those of the Belgian Army. The blown bridge presented an immediate obstacle to the paras' goal – reaching Fort Eben Emael and participating in the attack there. Attempts to cross the river resulted in Maier's death from enemy fire, but ultimately his second-in-command, Obergefreiter P. Meier, crossed the river, stole a bicycle and made it to the fort. There he reported to the Fallschirmjäger, before heading back to his unit around the Kanne bridge. Although he didn't actually find his unit again that day, he personally took some 110 Belgians prisoner, in what proved to be a highly eventful day for the young soldier (Gukeison 1993: 41).

While the Kanne experience proved to be an ordeal for Sturmgruppe 'Eisen', the paras at the other two bridges were enjoying a far higher degree of success. A key ingredient of this success was the attention the Luftwaffe was giving to Belgian command posts around Lanaken. Mrazek vividly described what happened:

> Commandant Giddeloo [sic] who was charged with the bridges at Veldwezelt and Vroenhoven, had his headquarters at Lanaeken [sic]. His location was apparently well-known to the Luftwaffe through German intelligence. Giddeloo was promptly informed by one of his observers in an outpost along the canal that the Germans were landing near one of the bridges. Just as word reached him, four Stuka, one by one, peeled off from formation high above Lanaeken and one after the other dived unerringly at Giddeloo's headquarters, releasing their bombs. Their aim was perfect, undoubtedly sharpened by months of practice for just this one mission, and the headquarters disintegrated under the force of the explosions. Giddeloo and twenty Belgians were blown apart just as he began to transmit orders to the guard at the bridges. (Mrazek 1972: 139)

The precision strikes against the Lanaken HQ, plus the lack of command initiative around the bridges themselves, would work heavily in favour of the German assault. Sturmgruppe 'Beton' touched down around Vroenhoven bridge at 0415hrs, one glider short after a towrope snapped on the inbound journey. Another glider was also struck by anti-aircraft fire on the way in, causing it to make a thumping crash-landing that seriously injured three men. Other groups of paras were straight into action, however, moving swiftly towards the bunker from which the demolition charges could be ignited. A Gefreiter Stenzel burst into the bunker, overcoming the resistance and cutting the wires that led out to the explosive blocks on the bridge's girders.

The bridge was safe, but this accomplishment was just the beginning of a long day for the Fallschirmjäger at Vroenhoven. Three squads were established at each end of the bridge, awaiting the Belgian counter-attacks that could come from virtually any direction. Counter-attacks rolled in throughout the day, but thankfully for the paras they received various reinforcements. These included more paratroopers, who conducted a parachute drop over the canal; unfortunately, two men died during the drop, one from enemy fire and one from drowning, after he landed in the waterway and became entangled in his parachute lines. Further support came from the precision air strikes of Ju 87 Stukas, which pounded the approach routes to the bridge, and the guns of an advanced Flak unit, which gave the paratroopers a source of heavy fire during a testing afternoon. By 2040hrs, when the paratroopers were finally able to

The attack on Veldwezelt Bridge (overleaf)

Men of Sturmgruppe 'Stahl' ('Steel'), commanded by Oberleutnant Gustav Altmann, attack the bridge at Veldwezelt in the early-morning hours of 10 May 1940. The gliders allocated for this particular bridge assault were heavily dispersed during the landing phase, some troops having to march as much as 1km to reach their objective. Here we see some of the first elements to begin the assault, attacking Bunker N at the western end of the bridge. The Fallschirmjäger advance with small-arms fire from their MP 40 submachine guns and Kar 98k carbines, hurling stick grenades against the bunker's apertures. The Belgian occupants of the bunker replied with machine-gun fire, but were eventually silenced by German demolition charges. Poor command-and-control structures meant the Belgians lost the opportunity to demolish the bridge when the German assault first began; here German paras with cutting equipment climb down onto the girders of the bridge, severing the control wires running down to the demolition charges.

pull off the bridge, their objective was securely in the hands of German forces. Sturmgruppe 'Beton' had lost seven dead and 24 wounded, against Belgian casualties numbering in the hundreds.

The action at Veldwezelt was of equal drama to that taking place at the other two bridges, and the Fallschirmjäger there would pay a heavier price in blood than at the other two bridge objectives. Again, the landing site plus the weather conditions forced the gliders to disperse around the bridge, some as much as a kilometre away. Initial losses were also taken when the glider carrying Trupp 3 made a heavy crash-landing, injuring almost all of the occupants of the aircraft. Those paratroopers close to the bridge, however, immediately attacked two key positions: Bunker N at the western end of the bridge, on the road level, and Bunker C beneath, which actually formed part of the support structure for the bridge's main girders. The paras were particularly fortunate in that the Belgian officers manning the bridge had actually contemplated blowing up the structure at the first alert to German invasion. Only the overruling command of a senior officer present, plus the Luftwaffe's precision strikes at Lanaken, prevented the bridge going the same way as that at Kanne.

A group of paras assaulted Bunker N with high-explosive demolition charges, as they stormed forward into small-arms fire. The German troops showed no mercy during this initial attack – 12 men from the Escadron des Cyclistes-Frontière du Limbourg died in a huge blast. Bunker C was also hit by explosive charges, which effectively sealed the position's doors tight, trapping the men inside. Other troops climbed onto the bridge's girders, cutting the wires that led to the demolition charges. Within just ten minutes

Here German forces cross the bridge at Veldwezelt, captured previously by the German airborne troops. At the far end of the bridge we can see Bunker N, while beneath the bridge, set as part of the pile, is Bunker C. (National Archives and Records Administration)

of the first gliders touching down around Veldwezelt, another crossing of the Albert Canal was in German hands.

The business of defending their gains was then put into action. Both sides of the bridge were made ready for the inevitable Belgian counter-attacks, which Ju 87s did their best to disrupt with predatory air attacks. Airborne reinforcements came in the form of two parachute-deployed machine-gun teams, which added critical additional firepower. The Belgians did indeed launch major attempts to retake the precious bridge, particularly around 0800hrs. Yet the combined attrition of the Stuka attacks, fire from the paras' own weapons plus the further support of the Flak unit, meant that the assaults did little but increase the level of Belgian casualties. The Fallschirmjäger hung on until the early evening, by which time forward German ground forces had reached the bridge and relieved the hard-pressed paras. Sturmgruppe 'Stahl' had, however, taken eight dead and 30 wounded, 14 of the wounded with severe injuries. Although the Belgian forces at and around the bridge suffered 110 dead and 200 POWs, as a proportion of the attack force the casualties of Sturmgruppe 'Stahl' had been heavy indeed. One point to note is that the Belgians trapped in Bunker C remained there until 1100hrs the next day, when German Pioniere finally levered open the buckled doors and released them straight into captivity.

Securing Eben Emael

By mid-morning on 10 May, the fortress of Eben Emael was already effectively humbled by a remarkable deployment of equally remarkable men. Most of the major guns were silent, especially those that could threaten the crucial bridges to the north. Visé 2 occasionally let off a shell, but it was focused to the south, and therefore couldn't really accomplish anything that threatened further German plans on the ground.

Conditions for the soldiers below ground were also far from promising. Many men had suffered wounds, and the Belgian medical personnel were doing their best to treat the injuries under poor lighting and in insanitary, damp rooms. Water was in short supply. Moreover, the garrison was stricken with a sense of the unknown, unable to tell how the broader fighting was going and whether their country as a whole was succumbing to the invaders.

There were nevertheless internal threats remaining, and some fighting to be done before Eben Emael would ultimately surrender. The fact was that the Belgian garrison below ground was still far greater in manpower than the 60 or so Germans active on the surface, and they were not yet out of fight.

There was also much uncertainty for Witzig's men. They had by now been awake since around 0200hrs, having had precious little sleep beforehand. They had taken casualties, and were also running low on water. Despite the airdrops from the He 111s, ammunition was also in short supply, and there was little hard information about when the ground troops would arrive as their relief. There was the very real prospect that the Belgians might make a major and co-ordinated counter-attack that would take back all that the Fallschirmjäger had so far gained.

The entrance to Eben Emael fortress as it is seen today. The roadway into the fortress included a retractable section that when deployed created a 4m-deep drop to prevent enemy vehicles and troops from passing through. (Scargill)

Jottrand was aware of this fact by now, and was resolutely putting together plans to retake his fortress. He radioed for artillery support from the neighbouring fortresses at Pontisse and Barchon, and soon shells were falling on the surface of Eben Emael among the German troops. Furthermore, Coupole Sud, which was still operational, also began to add its firepower against the interlopers, the gunners showing persistent defiance. Increasingly, the Germans had to take cover in captured emplacements.

Jottrand's hand was also strengthened a little by reinforcements arriving at Eben Emael from Wonck, but these men were not in the best condition or numbers, as the fortress chaplain's diary makes clear:

> Through the periscope of Bloc 1's machine gun, many soldiers can be seen arriving in twos and threes at the front gate of the fort from Wonck. They are being let in and arrive, totally deadbeat. It took them three, four hours along a road that would normally take them 30 minutes. All along the way they have suffered bombing and strafing … I go to the gate to welcome those who are coming in. Some are weeping from exhaustion. As soon as they get in, they fall to the ground in a heap, refusing to move … I settle them down and tell them to rest for a few hours. For the time being no one knows what to do with them anyway and besides, they are unable to do anything at the moment. (Quoted in Dunstan 2005: 52)

The depredation the Belgian troops had suffered during the journey up from Wonck only became fully apparent later. Some 233 men left Wonck at

1345hrs, but they were immediately spotted by Ju 87s and other Luftwaffe aircraft, which gave the troops constant attention. Dozens of men were killed or wounded by bombs or strafing attacks, and progress was painfully slow as they had to constantly seek cover. Many men fell away, unwilling to risk their lives further. The attrition was such that only 15 men of the original contingent made it to the fort (Gukeison 2005: 43).

Despite the reinforcements, Jottrand was never able to put together a decisive counter-attack, and the brave attempts that were made usually led to nothing but more casualties. The forces at his disposal had little experience in putting together fast infantry-style assaults, and their morale was already seriously weakened by the dominance of the German forces during the early hours of the operation in the West. Kurt Engelmann continues the story of this part of the day:

Heavy gunfire broke out in the south-west of the fort shortly after 1200hrs. Oberleutnant Witzig ordered [Ober]Feldwebel Wenzel to move up with some men, but they were unable to locate the enemy in the difficult terrain. For a short time we had to take cover in Trupp 3's Casemate 12 [Maastricht 1], as the fire became heavier and heavier. Feldwebel Wenzel was at this time wounded by a bullet, which grazed his head. Several times we had to move against the Belgians in the vicinity of Oberjäger Arendt's Casemate 12, as fresh troops had been moved up from Wonck. Although we suffered some losses, the Belgians were unable to make a successful coordinated attack. The shooting had stopped in this area after 1700hrs and Feldwebel Wenzel deployed his further depleted Trupp to the defensive position at the northern rampart, particularly as it was becoming dark and it was uncertain whether the Belgians would launch a counter-attack on the fort. All of us were extremely nervous in the dark, everyone stared into the darkness with their weapons at the ready, expecting an attack at any minute. Some artillery began firing at about 2100hrs, but we were lucky and we did not suffer any further losses. (Quoted in Dunstan 2005: 56)

German combat engineers prepare to make a river crossing. Pionier-Bataillon 51 made several dangerous crossings of the Albert Canal in such boats as it moved to link up with Sturmgruppe 'Granit' on 11 May 1940. Once the engineers reached the fortress, their skills in demolition and assault were put to good use. (National Archives and Records Administration)

By early evening, the Fallschirmjäger were aware that other German forces were nearby and trying to reach them, in the form of Pionier-Bataillon 51, commanded by Oberstleutnant Hans Mikosch. The advance elements of the battalion began to reach the Albert Canal around Kanne during the late afternoon, and a platoon attempted crossings of the canal in special rubber assault boats. These attempts were brought to a terrifying halt by blistering Belgian fire from the opposite bank.

Much of the fire was coming from Canal Nord. Witzig by this time could actually see the engineers attempting to make the crossing, and so decided to act against the blockhouse. Trupp 6, led by Oberjäger Harlos, was sent to attack the blockhouse, but its precipitous position – it was located 30m below the surface level of the fort – meant that it could not be approached directly. As a solution, Harlos and his men tied 50kg charges together and lowered them on ropes down to the blockhouse, detonating them just outside the bunker wall. The attack method had little success; as pointed out earlier, the power of a shaped charge is seriously weakened by any intervening distance between it and the target. (It is for this reason that we today see armoured vehicles clad in protective tubular cages. The cages serve to detonate shaped-charge RPG warheads before they actually impact on the vehicle's armour.) While the explosions must have certainly caused the occupants of the blockhouse some severe headaches, and possibly overpressure injuries, the position continued to pour its fire across the canal.

It was becoming steadily apparent that the canal would not be crossed in daylight, so the engineers waited until darkness before moving their boats up to a different crossing point, this time opposite the northern tip of the fortress. Despite the shroud of night-time, the German combat engineers were once again spotted on the water. They drove their paddles furiously to cross the canal, the surface of which was erupting from the impacts of bullet and shell. Nevertheless, they made it across in one piece, and then began to advance towards the northwest perimeter of the fortress. During the night, the Pionier platoon passed across the outer defences of the fortress and joined the Fallschirmjäger in the operations within the fortress.

The main body of Pioniere was also well on its way to Eben Emael. After his battalion managed to force a crossing of the canal at Kanne around dusk, Mikosch shuttled his heavy weapons across the waterway during the hours of darkness; he then moved his artillery up and positioned it to provide intense direct fire against the southwest corner of the fort once daylight broke the next day.

The night of 10/11 May was a restless one for both the defenders and the attackers. Witzig wanted to keep up pressure on the garrison below ground, and did so by dropping large explosive charges down the shafts of many emplacements, causing huge underground detonations. The engineers also began to add their explosive talents, and in some places the combined girder/door/sandbag barriers were blown down, meaning that the Germans could now gain access to the interior of the fortress. Blasts of automatic fire along the passageways reinforced the message that the German troops were in control. Although direct casualties from these attacks were relatively few, they caused a further drop in the already tenuous morale of the Belgian defenders. Not only that, but the fumes from the explosions began to filter through the corridors. The air conditioning systems of the fortress had already broken down, and containers of chloride-of-lime disinfectant had been smashed open, producing lethal chlorine fumes, so there was the real risk that the Belgians might simply choke to death. Jottrand sensibly began burning official papers in the fortress command post.

Surrender

The early morning hours of 11 May saw the final acts of the battle for Eben Emael. There was still some sporadic fire from the fortress, principally from Coupole Sud and Canal Nord. The latter was eventually destroyed by German gunfire from the opposite bank and a demolition attack by the German combat engineers. Yet to their credit many Belgian troops displayed admirable courage and tenacity during these last phases of the battle. Troops in emplacements in the west walls engaged in heavy gun battles with Mikosch's anti-tank weapons. Many stayed at their posts despite having no electricity and running low on ammunition, only abandoning their positions either when ordered to do so or when they no longer had anything to fire at their enemy.

Jottrand himself provided some inspiration to his men. He patrolled the smoke-filled corridors constantly, if only to gain an accurate impression of what was happening, to cut through the circulation of rumour and guesswork. He initially harboured ideas of mounting another counter-attack,

1215hrs, 11 MAY 1940

Eben Emael surrenders

A view from EBEN 1, atop Bloc 01, looking across the Albert Canal and Lanaye locks. This perspective illustrates how important it was for the German paras to 'blind' the observation domes at Eben Emael, as these provided the eyes for fire control along the Albert Canal and into the Netherlands. (Simon Dunstan)

but as the morning wore on the reality of the situation was undeniable. Wounded littered the corridors, and many would need urgent assistance if they were not to turn into fatalities. Although many of his courageous lieutenants remained at the fire-direction centre, there were fewer and fewer guns to fire. Moreover, it was clear that the German forces were penetrating deeper into the fortress. The Belgian defenders at the internal barricades were beginning to crumble, and an attempt to reinforce them saw many of the chosen troops fade away to hiding places with the fortress.

By this point it should be noted that Witzig's men had been officially relieved by Mikosch's Pioniere. Witzig's exhausted men rejoiced in the near-certainty of the eventual victory they had secured, and those that could marched out of the fortress with heads held high, as Engelmann recounts:

> We finally reached the entrance position and were able to take a short break. Some men rushed into the destroyed village [Eben Emael], searched a bar and found the water that we had been longing for. We quickly quenched our thirst and took as much as we could for our wounded and other comrades. We continued along the canal with the wounded transported some of the way on inflatable boats. We became soaked when we had to wade part of the way through the floods. We were then attacked by French bombers and since there was no cover we had to throw ourselves flat to the ground. Fortunately for us the bombs fell into the water about 40m away from us. We then continued towards the village of Kanne, where we handed our wounded over to the medics at the dressing station. (Quoted in Dunstan 2005: 57)

Engelmann goes on to explain that there was little rest for the paratroopers, who must have reached the outer limits of human endurance. They had to march for two hours to Maastricht, and spent the night sleeping on the hard wooden benches of a local school. They finally received vehicular transport, in the form of trucks, on the morning of the 12th, at which point 'we received our first cup of coffee, what a pleasure!' An attack by British bombers delayed the continuation of the journey, but by the evening they were back on German territory, where they were feted as heroes.

Back on 11 May, with the Pioniere in control of Eben Emael, Jottrand had reached the point of no return. A request to headquarters at Liège for the reinforcements to support a counter-attack came to nothing. A later conversation between Jottrand, Lieutenant-Général Joseph-Hubert-Godefroid de Krahe (3e Corps commander) and Général Jadot (Eben Emael's artillery commander) saw all three men hedging around the issue of surrender, even though that was now clearly the only way ahead. In the end, the decision was passed into Jottrand's hands alone, for no one else wanted the onerous responsibility of surrendering Belgium's most powerful fortification.

Jottrand gathered a council of defence together, consisting of the fortification's most senior officers, then confronted them with Article 51 of the fort's official defence policy, which dealt with the issue of surrender:

> The surrender of a fort is not justified unless it finds itself in one of the two following circumstances:

1. When all defensive means of the fort and of its personnel are useless and nonreparable.

2. When all means of subsistence of the garrison are exhausted. (Quoted in Mrazek 1972: 156)

Having read out the passage, Jottrand then asked the assembled company which policy they favoured – continued resistance or surrender. To Jottrand's surprise, given the past resistance of the gathered individuals, they all chose surrender. Understandably, they doubtless perceived that their country as a whole was under attack from an enemy whose strength far surpassed their own.

There now began the process of arranging the surrender. It was a prolonged and often confused process, drawn out to allow Jottrand and his men time to destroy as much as they could of the fortification. The generators were destroyed with dynamite charges, and other electrical and mechanical components were smashed up by hand with iron bars and axes. Any guns that remained in action had explosive charges pushed into the breech and detonated.

Finally, at about 1215hrs, a Belgian bugler sounded a surrender call on his instrument, the strange sound heard by Germans and Belgians alike. A Capitaine Vamecq, tasked with performing the formal surrender, emerged with another officer, who was holding a white flag. They approached the gated entrance to the fortification, and Vamecq went ahead. The fortress chaplain then noted what happened:

Captain Vamecq, ordered to negotiate the surrender, heads for the entrance of the fort escorted by a private holding a white flag but the Germans keep firing. A second attempt gets a better result. The firing ceases and negotiations begin. It takes some time before he returns. Unconditional surrender has been demanded. German soldiers approach the fort. The garrison is ordered to lay down their arms and to form ranks four abreast to leave the fort with officers in front. The medical personnel are to stay with the wounded. They will be looked after later on. While the men get rid of their weapons and form ranks we stay at the crossroads of the underground galleries. I shake hands with all those passing by. Slowly the column leaves the fort, which now becomes silent. (Quoted in Dunstan 2005: 56)

Eben Emael had fallen. By 28 May, the Belgian Army in its entirety had surrendered, and the Germans surged onwards in their campaign to take Western Europe.

ANALYSIS

Hindsight can make the German victory at Eben Emael appear almost inevitable. The sheer skill of the German attack force, plus the grave mistakes of the Belgian defence, make the victory appear like that of an eagle amid a flock of doves. Yet for those conducting the operation, without the clear view of the road ahead, the action was one that could have tipped against the Fallschirmjäger within a matter of minutes. Luck, as much as judgement, played a critical role in the victory for the Germans that day.

Taking the broad view, the victory at Eben Emael and against the bridges was undoubtedly remarkable. Eben Emael fortress was designed to resist the thrust of an entire army, but fewer than 90 men subdued it in a matter of hours. In fact, the Fallschirmjäger gained dominance only 30 minutes after touching down, as key casemates were destroyed and the fortress's garrison became confined to the gloomy and insular world of the tunnels and rooms down below. In total, Belgian losses were 23 dead and 59 wounded, against Witzig's losses of six dead and 15 wounded. These figures in themselves bear some consideration. Although the actual number of Witzig's casualties was incredibly small given the scale of the opponent, they still constituted just under 25 per cent of Sturmgruppe 'Granit'. It would not have taken many more casualties to have rendered the force combat ineffective.

So what were the deciding factors in the fall of Eben Emael? One aspect that needs explaining is why the Belgian forces didn't bring the fortress's immense firepower to bear upon the German deployment within the first few minutes of the assault. The assault on Eben Emael was at its most fragile in its opening minutes. If the anti-aircraft systems had been brought into play effectively, and shot up what were essentially fragile, low-level and slow-moving targets, then the combat power of Sturmgruppe 'Granit' could have been shredded even before the force touched down. Moreover, the machine guns of Mi-Sud and Mi-Nord, plus canister-round-armed 75mm weapons, had the potential to devastate the exposed paras in a whirlwind of crossfire.

Neither of these possibilities happened. Crucially, ammunition for all these positions was either inaccessible, available in only limited quantities or held in unopened ammunition boxes. The delay in acquiring and loading ammunition, therefore, provided a window of opportunity for the Fallschirmjäger to land safely, exit their gliders and storm the key emplacements. Jottrand also diverted essential troops away from their gun positions to assist with the demolition of the administrative buildings outside Bloc 1, when they could have been put to better use manning the very positions that could have saved the fortress. From this perspective, the inefficiencies of the Belgian defence were central factors in allowing Sturmgruppe 'Granit' to make a successful deployment in the first place. The problems here were compounded at several other levels. By sounding the *Attaque générale* when the fort was assaulted, rather than the *Attaque massif*, the focus of the defenders was skewed in entirely the wrong direction, looking outwards from the perimeter rather than focusing on the threat within the fortress itself. The failure to fire the general alert from the guns also meant that reinforcements were not rushed in promptly, something that could have tipped the battle in its early stages, although control of the garrison's troops dispersed outside the fortress walls appeared weak, despite the war footing upon which Belgium was placed. Furthermore, as we have seen Eben Emael was hobbled by an overcomplicated system of command and control, the decision-making process snaking out to various different headquarters through multiple figures. Such a labyrinthine process acted like a sea anchor on rapid decision-making, of the type that was required to respond to the fast-moving Fallschirmjäger. Jottrand was constrained in his reactions by having to run decisions past distant authorities, many of whom were not available during the confusion of those early hours of the German campaign in the West. Gukeison notes that 'Major Jottrand did not have decisive command and control of the fort, or the ability to communicate with surrounding ground support units. He was required to request approval from Liege for assistance from those ground support units' (Gukeison 1993: 59). A similar problem also confronted the Belgian troops based around the Vroenhoven and Veldwezelt bridges, hence their failure to implement the rapid demolition put into action at the Kanne bridge.

There were further problems for the Belgian defenders. The garrison, by being composed mainly of artillerymen and administrative staff, was essentially *strategic* in its outlook, and didn't have the necessary *tactical* training to take on the paras in an action of manoeuvre and decision. Because of this, we must give genuine credit to the many Belgian troops who did fight bravely over the course of those two days in May; it takes a rare man to keep fighting against a clearly superior enemy. Jottrand was also tireless in his pursuit of a counter-attack and recapture of the fort, at least until circumstances and general opinion forced a final surrender.

German paratroopers rush into action with small arms. The airborne operations involved in *Fall Gelb* seemed to provide a perfect validation of the Fallschirmjäger rationale, and Hitler enthusiastically looked for new opportunities to use his elite force. (Cody Images)

Eben Emael was not the only fortress assault conducted by German troops during the operations of spring 1940. Here a group of German infantry move across rough ground during an attack on Fort Boncelles, just to the southeast of Liège. (Cody Images)

The Belgian forces at Eben Emael should not be judged too harshly for the lapses in response, training and judgement, least of all by people who didn't have to face the terrifying threat from the skies on 10 May 1940. The troops were clear victims of pre-war under-investment. Having created a fortress of undeniable potency, the Belgian high command then allowed its full potential to weaken. Its garrison numbers dropped well below those optimal for defence, and its infrastructure did not receive the updates or maintenance necessary to maintain morale and its defensive integrity. Simon Dunstan has noted, for example, that the 'simple expedient of installing lengths of scrap railway lines vertically in the top surface of the fortress would have forestalled any attack by gliders at a cost of a few thousand Belgian Francs' (Dunstan 2005: 61). Airborne warfare was in its infancy, so this measure would have undoubtedly required some foresight. Yet the experiments in airborne warfare, the existence of combat gliders and application of para deployments in Scandinavia would all have been known to the high command. Had it been more energetically committed to maintaining the vigour of its defences, it might have prevented the fall of Eben Emael with nothing more than a few pieces of steel or wood.

On balance, the blame for under-investment cannot be laid entirely at Belgium's door. The French government had actually poured vast amounts of money – a full 80 per cent of construction costs – into the development of the fortress. When Belgium declared its neutrality in 1939, however, all such external funding came to an abrupt end. Belgium was hardly rolling in money since the end of World War I, a conflict that had laid waste to large tracts of Belgian land and much of Belgium's economy, so defence-spending allocations fell short of the ideal. Neutrality itself was also a contributor to the rapid Belgian collapse. The Belgian focus was on staying out of the gathering storm, yet given recent history that was surely a forlorn hope, whatever reassurances might come from elsewhere.

All these factors bred a Belgian garrison with desperately poor morale, and all the problems that come with that state of mind. In fact, being sent for service in Eben Emael was virtually regarded as a punishment posting by the troops. The lack of entertainment nearby, and the soulless underground living (the men could spend 170 straight hours underground before being allowed to come to the surface), bred a desertion rate of 10 per cent. Jottrand tried to combat this as best he could, by encouraging sport at the fortress, but it was insufficient to meet the needs of an unhappy force. Good morale energizes a soldiery, making it invest in its skills and steel itself for action. Poor morale, by contrast, insidiously spreads fatalism and reduces readiness, and such factors were apparent during the Eben Emael action.

Lightning attack

There is no getting away from the conclusion, therefore, that failings in the Belgian military system were central to the fall of Eben Emael. But conversely, there is also no denying that the Belgian troops were faced with elite troops executing a brilliantly conceived raid. Virtually everything about the German delivery of the raid at Eben Emael follows textbook models of planning and execution.

First, investment in training was extremely high, even before Hitler gave Student his commission to attack Eben Emael. Each para was given rigorous instruction in every aspect of tactical warfare, from co-ordinated unit movement through to handling demolitions, as well as in the skills of airborne deployment that separated the Fallschirmjäger from the rest of the German soldiery. They were fortunate to be riding the wave of Germany's massive 1930s rearmament programme, and the results included extremely high levels of morale and motivation, plus the inner conviction that comes from being a member of an elite. Recent combat experience in Poland, Norway and Denmark, although not unanimously successful, reinforced the sense of prowess. Moreover, the Fallschirmjäger were imbued with the military philosophy of *Auftragstaktik* (mission tactics) prevalent in the Wehrmacht at this time. *Auftragstaktik* emphasized the importance of subordinates being able to show initiative and leadership in the absence of a higher leadership. In essence, this ensured that if a leader were killed, wounded or otherwise taken out of the battlefield equation, those below him would still have the confidence and knowledge to maintain the mission. Nowhere was this better illustrated at Eben Emael than when Helmut Wenzel took over effective command of the raid when Witzig's glider cable snapped during the towing phase of the operation. Even though the raid's commander was not present on the battlefield, at least in the first few hours, the operation continued as normal, and the individual teams and their leaders continued to show initiative throughout the battle.

Student, Koch, Witzig and others took the Fallschirmjäger's powerful mindset and allied it to excellent intelligence and first-rate tactics. Nothing was left to chance, and every tactical decision was ruthlessly tested in exercises against similar fortifications. Every man in every team knew exactly what was expected of him on the ground and had a precise and focused objective, with appropriate allocations of weaponry. This meant that each individual attack had speed and complete focus, the Germans therefore dictating the tempo of the battle from the outset, and leaving the Belgians destabilized and uncertain.

Tactically, Student and Koch also made all the right decisions. Their first priorities were to knock out any positions that could threaten the troops who had landed on the top of the fortress plus those emplacements that could fire upon the key bridges to the north. Once these objectives had been fulfilled, which they were at a stunning pace, the Fallschirmjäger were then able to focus on keeping the fortress's garrison confined underground, thereby nullifying its huge advantages in numbers. The paras quickly knocked out many of the fort's observation positions, 'blinding' the men down below and

A famous image of the men of Sturmgruppe 'Granit' following the successful conclusion of the Eben Emael raid. The Fallschirmjäger provided the perfect material for early-war German propaganda, and were used to suggest the clear superiority of German troops over 'inferior' foreign opponents. (Cody Images)

injecting further uncertainty and confusion into their actions. The paras' co-ordination with air support, in the form of Ju 87 dive-bombing missions, meant that Belgian reinforcements moving up to Eben Emael were quickly scattered and weakened, cutting off Jottrand's men from external support. Air support such as this was also a deciding factor at some of the bridge actions, the Stukas giving the lightly armed Fallschirmjäger their own form of 'flying artillery'.

Sturmgruppe 'Granit' perfectly matched its strengths to the enemy weaknesses, and was therefore able to stay on top of the action from the outset. It also utilized the advantages of two new pieces of technology – the assault glider and the hollow charge. Taking the former first, we cannot underestimate the shock effect of the airborne assault on the Belgian troops who first encountered it. They were on the receiving end of the first gliderborne attack in history. The sight of those opening moments of the action must have been surreal for them. Large, silent aircraft, devoid of markings, suddenly appeared from out of the morning mist and landed just metres away from their positions. Then, from out of the gliders, came troops firing small arms and carrying demolitions. For those who had grown accustomed to the fortress being a place of boredom and routine, the sight must have been a challenge to understand, let alone respond to. The gliders gave the Fallschirmjäger the perfect means to deploy precisely on an otherwise inaccessible target area.

The hollow-charge weapons, meanwhile, provided the force to crack open many of the otherwise impenetrable casemates. However, on many occasions the hollow-charge demolition devices, and particularly the 50kg weapons, failed to punch through some of the most substantial structures. If anything, the most effective charges were the smaller types, pushed into gun barrels, wedged into gun ports or dropped down internal shafts. Although there was some disappointment over this performance, in fact the problem was that the technical understanding of how shaped charges worked was still in its infancy, particularly in regard to the relationship between cavity dimensions and armour penetration. Shaped charges were still far more effective than the conventional explosives for punching through armoured structures. Therefore many emplacements or structures in which the Belgian soldiers previously felt safe were rent open by the focused stream of molten metal and gas. Armour and ferro-concrete depth no longer gave the protection which they previously bestowed.

Ultimately, Witzig himself gave what he saw as the reasons for the victory at Eben Emael:

There are three main reasons:

a) The shattered morale of the garrison, linked to the fear that we were already inside the casemates.

b) The weakening of the fortress defences caused by the loss of a number of the defensive posts, and the apparent uncertainty attached to which posts had been lost and whether the outer defences were holding.

c) The lack of support – other than of indirect artillery support – and of reinforcement from outside. Because of this it was not possible to mount a strong counter-attack. 40 infantrymen were sent into one counter-attack: of these only 12 survived. (Quoted in Kühn 1978: 37)

This terse list is entirely accurate. What it does not mention, but Witzig would doubtless have acknowledged, was the brilliance and courage of the men he sent into battle.

The heroes

On 11 May 1940, the *Wehrmachtbericht* (Armed Forces Report), a daily radio broadcast to the German armed services, laconically explained the victory at Eben Emael:

The strongest fort of the fortress Lüttich [Liège], Eben-Emael, which dominates the crossings of the Maas and Albert-Canal near and west of Maastricht surrendered Saturday afternoon. The commanding officer and 1,000 men were taken prisoner of war. The fort was already rendered defenceless and the garrison pinned down on 10 May by a specially selected unit of the Luftwaffe under the leadership of Oberleutnant Witzig and deploying new combat means. The garrison dropped their arms when an attacking unit of the Army, after heavy combat, established contact with the *Sturmgruppe Witzig*. (Anon n.d.: 144–45)

The commanders of the Eben Emael raid pose with Adolf Hitler, the newly received Knight's Cross decorations hanging around their necks. The photo was taken on 16 May 1940. Witzig is second from the left, Koch third from the left. (Cody Images)

This broadcast probably constituted the most restrained presentation of the action in Belgium. For a Nazi regime so keenly attuned to the possibilities of propaganda, the victory at Eben Emael was an unprecedented opportunity to lay claim to German superiority. The celebrations began soon after the Fallschirmjäger returned to Germany. A welcoming reception was held at Köln-Ostheim airbase on 12 May, and another at Münster the following day. This was held by General der Flieger Albert Kesselring, the commander of Luftflotte 2, who presented the paras with the Iron Cross 1st Class. Then on 16 May, after the paras had enjoyed two weeks of well-earned leave, Hitler met with the heroes at the Führerhauptquartier 'Felsennest' near Bonn. Here each officer of Sturmabteilung 'Koch' was given the Knight's Cross of the Iron Cross. Hitler proudly posed for photographs alongside the key figures of the raid, and the German newsreels and press dwelt on the details of both men and tactics for an appreciative public. There was even a series of postcards printed for sale, each featuring a picture of a significant figure from the raid.

Superlatives quickly stacked up around the Fallschirmjäger, and continued to do so after the war. Student himself declared, with some justification, that:

> It was a deed of exemplary daring and decisive significance. A handful of paratroops, with powerful support by the Air Force, forced a passage for an army to break through. I have studied the history of the last war and the battles on all fronts. But I have not been able to find anything among the host of brilliant actions – undertaken by friend or foe – that could be said to compare with the success achieved by Koch's assault group. (Quoted in Kühn 1978: 37)

It is not difficult to appreciate why the German leadership made so much of the victory at Eben Emael. It seemed a perfect, clear-cut illustration of the superiority of German training and spirit over seemingly lesser enemies, and a vindication of the massive investment in the armed forces during the 1930s. The disparity between the size and strength of the objective, and those of the attacking force, gave a sense that for the German military anything was possible, a message more than reinforced by the subsequent German victory over the French and British in the West.

The contrast with the Belgian forces could not have been more striking. The mentally crushed garrison of Eben Emael first went into captivity, held in Fallingbostel POW camp in Germany. They were even kept isolated for six months, as the German authorities did not want them disseminating stories about the shaped-charge weapons used by the Fallschirmjäger. They were finally liberated by the Allies in 1945, but the subsequent inquiry into the fall of Eben Emael neatly blamed Jottrand and the garrison, sidestepping the failings of those higher up the chain of command.

CONCLUSION

In some ways, the victory at Eben Emael was a curse as well as a blessing for the Fallschirmjäger. In the same way that the breaking of the Iranian Embassy siege in London in 1980 produced unrealistic public expectations of the British Special Air Service, the German paratroopers were placed on a dangerous pedestal. Eben Emael was, in many ways, the perfect operational environment for the Fallschirmjäger. It involved a focused, sharply defined objective and a compact timeline for operations. It wasn't long, however, before the German leadership considered using the Fallschirmjäger on a far larger scale.

On 20 May 1941, Hitler launched *Unternehmen Merkur* (Operation *Mercury*), the airborne invasion of Crete. The contrast to the raid on Eben Emael could not have been more pronounced. A total of 22,750 paratroopers and airlanded soldiers were delivered by 500 transport aircraft and 80 gliders. This time, however, the British and Commonwealth enemy was both forewarned and well armed. On the first day of operations, the Germans managed to establish toeholds on the north of the island at the cost of hundreds of dead and wounded. One battalion alone lost 400 of its 600 men. Dozens of men were shot dead even as they floated down to earth. Sometimes Allied soldiers simply waited outside crash-landed gliders, methodically shooting each para as he emerged fatalistically from the glider door. Dozens of other paras drifted uncontrollably in their parachutes into the sea, where they drowned, or injured themselves landing on Crete's rocky surface.

Remarkably, Crete was indeed eventually taken by the Fallschirmjäger, but total German fatalities numbered more than 7,000. Hitler, and Student, were stunned by the losses. The operation clearly showed the limits and vulnerabilities of airborne deployments, and Hitler ensured that the paratroopers would never again make a drop on such a scale. Consequently, they largely became an elite infantry force, which subsequently paid an appalling cost fighting on the Eastern and Western Fronts, and in Italy.

Hitler presents the leaders of Sturmabteilung 'Koch' with their Knight's Cross decorations on 16 May 1940. Hitler's utter confidence in his Fallschirmjäger was reinforced by their actions in Greece in April 1941, but shattered by the losses of airborne troops during the battle of Crete only weeks later. (Cody Images)

Many of the paratroopers who had fought at Eben Emael in May 1940 would not see the end of the war. At least ten paratroopers from Sturmgruppe 'Granit' were killed on Crete alone. A further 20 would die in other actions, most of them on the Eastern Front, where the Fallschirmjäger were frequently used in a 'fire brigade' role, rushed to shore up faltering sectors from the worst of the Soviet onslaught. Many more of this elite group survived the war, but with the legacy of severe wounds.

The Fallschirmjäger, as with all of Germany's armed forces, paid a terrible price for Hitler's hubris between 1939 and 1945. Yet in May 1940, with the victory of Eben Emael fresh in their minds and in the public imagination, they must have felt unconquerable. Only subsequent fighting under very different circumstances would strip them of such illusions.

BIBLIOGRAPHY AND FURTHER READING

Anonymous (n.d.). *Die Wehrmachtberichte 1939–1945 Band*

Anonymous (1943). Canadian Army Training Memorandum No. 24, March 1943

Dunstan, Simon (2005). *Fort Eben Emael: The Key to Hitler's Victory in the West*. Oxford: Osprey Publishing

Gukeison, Thomas B. (1993). 'The Fall of Eben Emael: The Effects of Emerging Technologies on the Successful Completion of Military Objectives'. Unpublished MA thesis, Fort Leavenworth, KS

Kühn, Volkmar (1978). *German Paratroopers of World War II*. London: Ian Allan

Kurowski, Franz (2010). *Jump Into Hell: German Paratroopers in World War II*. Mechanicsburg, PA: Stackpole Books

Lucas, James (1988). *Storming Eagles: German Airborne Forces in World War II*. London: Arms & Armour Press

McNab, Chris (2000). *German Paratroopers: The Illustrated History of the Fallschirmjäger in World War II*. Minneapolis, MN: Motorbooks International

McRaven, William H. (1990). *Special Operations: Case Studies in Special Operations Warfare – Theory and Practice*. New York, NY: Presidio Press

Mrazek, James E. (1972). *Prelude to Dunkirk: The Fall of Eben Emael*. London: Robert Hale

Quarrie, Bruce (2001). *Fallschirmjäger: German Paratrooper 1935–45*. Oxford: Osprey Publishing

Rottman, Gordon (2006). *World War II Airborne Warfare Tactics*. Oxford: Osprey Publishing

INDEX

References to illustrations are shown in **bold**. Plates are shown with page in **bold** and the caption page in brackets, e.g. **27** (26).

aircraft, German
  DFS transport gliders 29–30, **31**, 35, 41–42, 54, 74
  Heinkel He 111 bombers 51
  Junkers Ju 52 transport aircraft **5**, 7, **15**, 30, 35, 37, 41–42, **43**
  Junkers Ju 87 Stuka dive-bombers 51, 59, 63, 65, 74
aircraft, Italian: Caproni Ca.73 aircraft 6–7
aircraft, Soviet: Tupolev TB-3 aircraft 7
Albert Canal **10**, 11, 12, 14, 19, 28, **36**, 56–63, **65**, 66, **67**
Alefs, Obergerfreiter, Wilhelm 41
Altmann, Oberleutnant Gustav 57
anti-aircraft guns 26
anti-tank guns 19, 20, 22, **39**
Arendt, Oberjäger Peter 40, 41, 48, 49, 50

Bassenge, Major Gerhard 7
Belgian army
  analysis 70–75
  bridges **48**, **51**, 56–63
  casualties of the raid 70
  the consolidation of the attack 51–56
  Coupole Nord 44–45
  equipment **13**, 34
  final defence of the fortress 63–67
  general alert 39–40
  Maastricht 1 and Maastricht 2 48–50
  Mi-Sud and Mi-Nord 45–48
  morale 38
  onset of the attack 42–43
  surrender 67–69
  troop numbers 39
  uniform 34
  weapons 34
Berry, Captain, Albert 4
Blitzkrieg (lightning war) 28
blockhouses 19–22, **55**
Bock, Generaloberst Fedor von 13
Boncelles fort 11, **72**
Bräuer, Major Bruno 7
Broadwick, Georgia 'Tiny' 5
Brünn Gew 33/40(t) rifles 16

C 60 L/50 anti-tank guns 22
Caproni Ca.73 aircraft 6–7
Commission d'Étude du Système des Fortifications (Commission for the Study of National Fortification) 11
Cremers, Maréchal des logis 54
Crete (1941) 15, 77–78
cupolas **20**, **23**, **24**, 33, 44–45, 51, **54**, 54–55, 56

Delica, Leutnant Egon 37, 50, 51
Denmark, invasion of (1940) 17–18
Deutsche Forschungsanstalt für Segelflug (German Research Institute for Sailplane Flight, DFS) 29
DFS transport gliders 29–30, **31**, 35, 41–42, **54**, 74
Drucks, Gefreiter Richard 50
Dyle Line 13

Eben Emael fort
  analysis of the raid 70–75
  armament 19–22

bridges **48**, **51**, 56–63
  the consolidation of the attack 51–56
  Coupole Nord 44–45
  details of the fort 18–27
  Maastricht 1 and Maastricht 2 48–50
  Mi-Sud and Mi-Nord 45–48
  origins of the raid 10–18
  the plan 28–37
  securing the fort 63–67
  surrender 67–69
Engelmann, Kurt 56, 65, 68

Fall Gelb (Case Yellow) 11–14, 28
Fallschirmjäger (paratroopers)
  analysis of the raid 70–75
  bridges **48**, **51**, 56–63
  casualties of the raid 70
  consolidating the attack 51–56
  Coupole Nord 44–45
  equipment **6**, 34
  forces assigned to Eben Emael area 32
  formation of the regiment 7–8
  the heroes 75–76
  Maastricht 1 and Maastricht 2 48–50
  Mi-Sud and Mi-Nord 45–48
  onset of the raid 38–43
  Operation *Mercury* (1941) 15, 77–78
  the plan 28–37
  securing the fortress 63–67
  surrender of the fortress 67–69
  the 'Ten Commandments' 16
  training **12**, 14–16, **15**, **17**, **31**, 33–37, 73
  uniform 15–16, 34
  weapons 16–17, **18**, 30–32, **31**, **32**, **34**, **51**, 57, 74
flamethrowers 16, **34**
FN 1930 Mle D rifles **34**
Föster, Max von 31
FRC Modèle 31 machine guns 22
Fusil-Mitrailleur 1930 (FM 30) machine guns 19

Gigon, Maréchal des logis 48, 49
Gigon, Hermann 7
grenades **34**

Haug, Erwin 43
Heidrich, Major Richard 8
Heinemann, Fritz 44
Heinkel He 111 bombers 51
Hitler, Adolf **71**, **75**, 76, 77, **78**
  Fall Gelb (Case Yellow) 11–14
  the plan 28, 29, 30, 33

Jacobs, Hans 29
Jadot, Général 68
Joiris, Maréchal des logis 44
Jottrand, Major Jean Fritz 27, 39, 40, 55, 58, 64, 65, 67–69, 71
Junkers Ju 52 transport aircraft **5**, 7, **15**, 30, 35, 37, 41–42, **43**
Junkers Ju 87 Stuka dive-bombers 51, 59, 63, 65, 74

Kanne bridge 56–59, **58**
Kar 98k carbines 16, **34**
Kesselring, General der Flieger Albert 76
Koch, Hauptmann Walter 9, 33, 73
Krahe, Lieutenant-Général Joseph-Hubert-Godefroid de 68

Lange, Unteroffizier Heiner 43
Lippisch, Dr Alexander 29
Luftwaffe, the 37, 41–42, 51, 65
Luger Pistole 08 16, **34**

M1889 rifles 34
machine guns 20, 22–24, **39**
Maginot Line 12
Manstein, Generalleutnant Erich von 13
Maxim MG 08 machine guns 19
Meeson, L. 42–43
MG 34 machine guns **31**
Mikosch, Oberstleutnant Hans 66
Mitchell, Brigadier General William 'Billy' 5
mortars 16
MP 38/MP 40 submachine guns 16, **18**, **34**

Netherlands (1940) **50**
Niedermeier, Hans 50, **51**
Norway, invasion of (1940) 17–18

Oberkommando des Heeres (OKH; Army High Command) 7
observation domes 22, 23, 24, 26, **51**, **57**
Operation *Mercury* (1941) 15, 77–78

parachutes, development of 7, 14
paratroopers *see* Fallschirmjäger (paratroopers)
Pershing, General John 5
PFL *(Position Fortifée de Liège)* 11, 12
Polizeiabteilung 'Wecke' (Police Detachment 'Wecke') 7
Position Fortifée de Liège (PFL) 11

Reichenau, Generaloberst Walther von 13

Sauer 7.65mm Modell 38(H) pistols 16
Schacht, Leutnant Gerhard 57
Schächter, Leutnant Martin 57
Schlieffen Plan 13
shaped charges 30–32, **32**, **34**, **51**, **57**, 74
Stever, Generalmajor Johann Joachim 37
Student, Generalmajor Kurt 8, 9, 14, 29, 30, 33, 73, 76, 77

Torreele, Colonel Albert 24
training **12**, 14–16, **15**, **17**, **31**, 33–37, 73
Tupolev TB-3 aircraft 7

uniform, Fallschirmjäger (paratroopers) 15–16, 34

Veldwezelt bridge 56–57, 59, **59**, **62**, 62–63
Versailles Treaty (1919) 7, 10, 29
Vroenhoven bridge 56–57, 59–62

Walther, Major Erich 17
weapons, Belgian army 34
weapons, Eben Emael fort 19–26, **39**
weapons, Fallschirmjäger (paratroopers) 16–17, 57
  grenades 34
  Kar 98k carbines **34**
  Luger Pistole 08 **34**
  MG 34 machine guns **31**
  MP 38/MP 40 submachine guns **18**, 34
  shaped charges 30–32, **32**, **34**, **51**, 74
Wenzel, Oberfeldwebel 45, 51, 54–55, 56
Witzig, Oberleutnant Walter **29**, 33, 35, 41, 56, 66, 68, 75
Wonck fort 11
World War I (1914–18) 4–5, 13